Surprised Again!

Praise for *Surprised Again!*

"Pollock and Adler masterfully track governments' financial response to the global pandemic—and raise critical questions about the future implications of increasing backstops for housing, student loans, pensions, and maybe even cryptocurrencies. A brilliant and clear recounting of the last two years, and a roadmap for the next potential crisis."

    —Winthrop Watson, President and CEO of the Federal Home Loan Bank of Pittsburgh

"Without warning the Covid-19 pandemic swept across the globe in early 2020, fundamentally altering the daily lives of billions. At the same time, the pandemic gave rise to a financial crisis that shocked experts and threw markets into a tailspin. This definitive account by two Treasury Department insiders provides critical insight into the causes of that crisis, how it was abated, and how we might be less surprised by the next one. Suffice it to say, it is a must-read book for economic policymakers, investment professionals, and anyone interested in financial markets."

    —Heath Tarbert, former Chairman, Commodity Futures Trading Commission

"What will not surprise you is the wisdom, wit, and insight that Alex Pollock and Howard Adler bring to this indispensable guide to financial prophecy. The future may be a closed book, but you must open—and read—this one."

    —James Grant, *Grant's Interest Rate Observer*

"Tired of government bailouts with taxpayer money? Want government programs designed to maximize benefits while minimizing costs to the public fisc? Thought about risk transfers associated with federal intervention in the market? Then read this book!"

    —Keith Noreika, former Acting Comptroller of the Currency

"*Surprised Again!* is an outstanding demonstration of how government efforts to promote financial stability can sow the seeds of instability. The surprise in question was the 2020 financial crisis caused by the Covid pandemic and lockdowns. The authors, Alex J. Pollock and Howard B. Adler—Treasury officials at the time—have given us a work of disinterested scholarship, filled with lucid explanations and eye-opening charts. They show that some of the government's responses successfully stabilized markets and alleviated immediate hardships, others failed to address serious problems the pandemic and lockdowns had exposed, and others produced new surprises (such as surging asset and price inflation) that left us ill-prepared for the next crisis—which, we now know, was to arrive in early 2022. *Surprised Again!* will demystify finance for students and give experts a deeper understanding of things they thought they knew."

—**Christopher DeMuth, Distinguished Fellow, Hudson Institute, and former President, American Enterprise Institute**

"*Surprised Again!* does a superb job of revisiting the financial meltdown, government response, and economic recovery triggered by the pandemic. The authors infuse this history with thoughtful reflections on the history of central bank crisis management and the political ramifications of the Federal Reserve and Congressional actions taken to combat the Covid crisis. In the end we learn what perhaps is no surprise: bailouts lead to bubbles, and politicians will never let a crisis go to waste."

—**Paul Kupiec, Senior Fellow, American Enterprise Institute**

"In *Surprised Again!* Alex Pollock and Howard Adler have created a true gem for the reader. At one level so easy to understand, at another deeply philosophical and rich in insights about the human condition in the environment of economics and finance. The reader will not find anywhere else such a lucid account of how the details of Fed and Treasury policies made the 'everything bubble.' The 'Cincinnatian doctrine' is a treasure to be unwrapped, and even the most crypto-illiterate amongst us will appreciate the authors' treatment of the revealed 'sting in the tail' of a crypto surprise: how what seemed like a libertarian revolt against central banks will very likely end up vastly increasing and centralizing their power. Join the trip of superior but humbled understanding of financial markets made possible by *Surprised Again!*"

—**Brendan Brown, Senior Fellow, Mises Institute and Senior Fellow, Hudson Institute**

"A masterful survey of the financial sector and its post-Covid dependence on easy money from the Federal Reserve. This book is the first place to turn for a clear exposition of key financial topics—housing, municipal debt, pension funds, student loans, cryptocurrencies, and more. The reader will be surprised yet again at the extent of financial problems lurking below the surface."

    —Thomas H. Stanton, Johns Hopkins University

"*Surprised Again!* is a salutary reminder that we do not see through the 'fog of human affairs,' and don't see when the next crisis is almost upon us, or understand it fully when it hits us. It hints that, as human beings, we do not want to recognize that hard times are coming. More important, the authors suggest that this is partly due to mistaken beliefs that economic laws are hard scientific laws. The authors carefully analyze the multiple sources of debt in the American economy, potential sources of debt crises, if not now, then in the future. They insightfully consider the risks of central banks seeking to extend their power by the introduction of central bank digital currency, possibly replacing commercial bank money."

    —Dr. Oonagh McDonald CBE, author of *Cryptocurrencies:
    Money, Trust and Regulation*

"From Covid and crypto to student loans, inflation, and the Federal Reserve, the authors of *Surprised Again!* puncture conventional thinking about finance, government, and our so-called free market economy with wit, logic, and a commanding understanding of our nature as animals subject to prolonged fits of irrationality, especially when it comes to money. Every member of Congress and everyone on the Federal Reserve Board should own a copy; we can even hope they read it."

    —Arthur Herman, Senior Fellow, Hudson Institute,
    and author of *The Viking Heart: How Scandinavians*
    Conquered the World*

"In the aftermath of the 2008 financial crisis I made two predictions: There would be another crisis; and it would be caused by something other than the originate to distribute mortgage system that abandoned any pretense of credit underwriting. Read this book if you want to understand why these predictions were right. It is a very accessible volume that explains eternal verities about financial institutions and markets: financial markets are inherently prone to periodic crises; government intervention has mitigated some of these tendencies, while other intervention, however well intentioned, has made things worse. The analysis is supported with readily understandable data about recent financial crises and the public policy responses. You do not need a degree in finance to understand it, and, for the most part, the data that is presented stand on their own and are not, as in so much current writing, provided as a prop for an ideological polemic."

—**Allan I. Mendelowitz, President,**
ACTUS Financial Research Foundation

"*Surprised Again!* is a highly sophisticated analysis of every major potential problem in the U.S. financial system today, presented in a delightfully readable and accessible form. The theme of the book is the surprise we have all experienced when a seemingly placid and functioning sector of the U.S. economy suddenly turns into a source of dangerous instability or crisis. Why do these things happen so often, and why don't we see them coming? The authors' high level positions in the U.S. Treasury Department put them in ideal positions to understand how difficult it can be—even with the informational resources of the U.S. government—to predict the future of the vast U.S. economy or financial system. So the lesson is clear: surprises can never be ruled out, but it is possible to understand where the most likely economic or financial dangers lurk. The authors lay these out with admirable clarity. Forewarned is forearmed."

—**Peter J. Wallison, Senior Fellow Emeritus,**
American Enterprise Institute

Surprised Again!

THE COVID CRISIS
AND THE
NEW MARKET BUBBLE

Alex J. Pollock
Howard B. Adler

PAUL DRY BOOKS
Philadelphia 2022

The authors express their special thanks to
Daniel Semelsberger, research assistant *extraordinaire*.

First Paul Dry Books Edition, 2022

Paul Dry Books, Inc.
Philadelphia, Pennsylvania
www.pauldrybooks.com

Printed in the United States of America

ISBN 978-1-58988-165-5

Library of Congress Control Number: 2022943839

To Anne's and my children and grandchildren—
may you have perspective and balance
as you encounter the surprises ahead.

AJP

To my wife and life partner Tanya,
whom I adore beyond all measure,
and to our daughter Alexa, a journalist of whom we
are both extraordinarily proud.

HBA

Contents

Surprised Again!

CHAPTER 1

Surprised Again!

W HEN THE AUTHORS of this book, Alex Pollock and Howard Adler, met in Howard's spacious office in the U.S. Treasury building in December 2019, we knew that financial crises occur on average about once a decade and that it had been ten years since the last one, the "Great Financial Crisis" of 2007–09. We knew that history featured these recurring financial crises, and the classic Treasury building had many times been the scene of tense and urgent efforts to address them. Both of us had responsibility to help the government's top-level Financial Stability Oversight Council, or "FSOC,"[1] anticipate possible future financial crises. So, although the economy was ending 2019 with strong momentum, we were thinking about whether and how another crisis might occur.

We also knew, as a fundamental truth, that the financial future is not only unknown, but unknowable. Alex had written a book with the subtitle, *Why We're Always Surprised*, showing that this both is and must be so.[2] Could we be heading for another financial crisis in 2020, one still hidden from us by the fog of the future?

At that point, we were not able, we agreed, to articulate a probable source of such a crisis. There was a long list of various macrofinancial worries, including asset price inflation, high levels of leveraged corporate loans, shifts from bank to nonbank lenders, concerns that credit rating agencies were not rigorous enough in rating structured debt products, and structural weaknesses in a housing finance system tied to Fannie Mae and Freddie Mac in seemingly endless government conservatorship. These seemed to suggest problems, but not crises. The emergence of a new pandemic was certainly not on the list of financial risk factors. The sobering pattern of financial history notwithstanding, it appeared to us that no crisis was looming.

"But," said Alex to Howard, "when the next crisis arrives, we won't see it coming." And so it turned out. Three months later, the crisis of 2020 arrived, financial markets went into panicked free fall, and we didn't see it coming. Neither did anyone else.

In 2020, the emergence of the extremely contagious Covid-19 virus in China turned into a global, intertwined health-political-economic-financial crisis. Given the unknowable nature of the financial future, it is not surprising that we were surprised, but we—and virtually everybody—were surprised yet again by the onset of the 2020 financial crisis.

Among the beliefs proven mistaken by this crisis was one expressed by a prominent central banker, Janet Yellen, who was then Chair of the Federal Reserve Board (as we write, she is Secretary of the Treasury): "Would I say there will never, ever be another financial crisis?" Yellen said in June 2017. "Probably that would be going too far. But I do think we are much safer, and I hope it will not be in our lifetimes. And I don't believe it will be."[3]

Yet the next crisis did come well within "our lifetimes," and her belief, in spite of all her experience and expertise, had been simply wrong. The time from Yellen's optimistic "lifetime" assessment to when the new financial crisis burst upon us was less than three years.

Similarly, this time from the private sector, we had the pronouncement of James Gorman, Chairman and CEO of the famous investment bank, Morgan Stanley, on the question of future financial crises. "The probability of it happening again in our lifetime is as close to zero as I can imagine," said he, in 2013.[4] But it did happen again. When financial markets panicked in March 2020, he was only 61 years old and still Chairman and CEO of Morgan Stanley, as he continues to be as we write. At age

61, he could statistically expect about two more decades of life—plenty of time for a couple more financial crises.

As Mr. Gorman's mistaken imagining makes clear, things that experts may imagine have a zero probability do nonetheless happen anyway. We cannot too often remind ourselves of and apply to our thinking about financial markets the dictum of physicist Freeman Dyson: "Many things that had once been unimaginable nevertheless came to pass." That they do come to pass reflects both the unknowable nature of future financial interactions and also the striking limits of our imagination, even when accompanied by high intelligence, demonstrated talent, and broad experience.

In support of her optimistic 2017 outlook, the then-Federal Reserve Chair took comfort from the fact that government officials "are doing a lot more to try to look for financial stability risks that may not be immediately apparent . . . in order to try to detect threats to financial stability that may be emerging."

Yes, they were indeed looking diligently, just as the authors were doing in December 2019. A great many intelligent, informed, responsible people around the world were looking for financial risks at the same time and writing long and graph-filled reports about their efforts. But when it comes to the financial future, it is much easier to look than to see. No one saw the risk that turned into catastrophic reality. The unimagined was suddenly upon us.

The 2007–09 "Great Financial Crisis" surprised financial experts just as the 2020 crisis did. About that crisis, former Federal Reserve Vice Chairman Donald Kohn said, with a candor unusual for the Federal Reserve, "Not only didn't we see it coming," but in the midst of it, "central bankers had trouble understanding what was happening."[5]

This is confirmed by international financial expert William White, who served in senior positions with the Organization for Economic Co-operation and Development, the Bank for International Settlements, and the Bank of Canada. Reflecting on the 2007–09 crisis, he wrote, "It is important to note that central banks and regulators failed to see the bust coming, just as they failed to anticipate its potential magnitude" and "None of the

large central banks, nor the IMF and the OECD, saw the downturn coming."[6]

They failed to see the crisis coming in spite of the fact that, as
the Bank for International Settlements reported in 2004,

> with financial stability rising to the top of national and
> international policy agendas, great efforts have been made
> at least since the mid-1980s [a time of multiple financial
> crises] to upgrade prudential safeguards. And these have
> been embedded into a broader strategy of strengthening
> the financial infrastructure. . . . Over time, prudential reg-
> ulation and supervision have become a core element of the
> so-called new "international financial architecture," built
> largely on the development and implementation of interna-
> tional standards.[7]

Three years after these pretty self-satisfied comments, they
were in the midst of another vast crisis and trying to figure out
what happened.

Henry Paulson, U.S. Secretary of the Treasury from 2006–
2009, in his memoir of that crisis, *On the Brink*, tells us how often
he was surprised by events. In particular, that the crisis "came
from an area we hadn't expected—housing—and the damage
it caused was much deeper and much longer lasting than any of
us could have imagined." That is, it was something they not only
did not, but could not, imagine. So, Paulson observes, "We had
no choice but to fly by the seat of our pants, making it up as we
went along."[8]

Reflecting on "the unknowable future," in a book written just
before the 2020 surprises burst on the scene, the former Governor of the Bank of England, Mervyn King, and co-author, John
Kay, rightly observed, based on long experience, that the world of
economics and finance is marked by "radical uncertainty" and "is
not governed by unchanging scientific laws." These distinguished
financial experts reach the sobering philosophical conclusion that
"often there will be no objectively right answer, either before or
after the event."[9]

In "The Big Lessons From History," financial writer Morgan Housel sums it up succinctly: "Risk is what you don't see," and "The riskiest stuff is always what you don't see coming." He is absolutely right. As another striking example, he cites Nobel laureate economist Robert Shiller, well known for his work on bubbles and irrational exuberance, to the effect that nobody forecast the Great Depression of the 1930s. "I have asked economic historians to give me the name of someone who predicted the depression," said Shiller, "and it comes up zero."[10]

During 2019, we were trying to do better than that, but didn't. As later counted by the U.S. Office of Financial Research, in 2019 there were no fewer than 30 different official financial stability reports issued by governments and central banks of advanced economies, and by multilateral organizations. (If you add emerging market countries, the Center for Financial Stability counts 60 such reports.) The world did not lack for reports or effort. These documents included the voluminous financial stability reports of the Financial Stability Oversight Council and the Office of Financial Research itself, both extensively reviewed by the distinguished members of FSOC and their expert staffs.

Of the 30 reports, as the OFR observed,[11] not a single one anticipated a financial crisis in 2020 or thought that there was a significant probability of one. They assessed the overall risks as "moderate." Not one discussed the potential for a new pandemic to create financial instability.

Yet in a broader context, the emergence of new, virulent viruses was well known to biology and medicine. That, over time, there was the possibility of frightening new pandemics had been frequently discussed and predicted. "This kind of pandemic was widely and insistently and repeatedly predicted," said historian Adam Tooze of Columbia University, adding that "what people had predicted was worse than the coronavirus."[12]

But that a new virus would lead to financial crisis was not in the least foreseen. No one imagined a disastrous link between the behavior of viruses as known to science and the panic that periodically besets financial markets.

Did you, Excellent Reader, imagine such a link in advance of the 2020 crisis? No, you didn't. Did you put even a tiny probability on it, as one of your financial "tail risks"? No, you didn't. You were, we guess, completely surprised again, along with the authors of this book and all the financial and economic experts.

To link the emergence in China of a new virus to international economic disaster and financial panic required forecasting an essential intermediate step: political actions. To control the spread of the pandemic, governments locked down huge sectors of the economy. However necessary those actions were, financial actors suddenly had to guess what the lockdowns meant for economic growth, employment, future cash flows, their present values, the prices of financial assets, and for defaults on debt, all of which had, a short while before, seemed so benign. Nobody knew; everybody feared the unknown.

All finance is political finance. The pervasive intertwining of finance with politics and government is one of the essential reasons why the financial future is fundamentally uncertain.

Of course, the events of 2020 were hardly the first demonstration that highly intelligent, knowledgeable people in positions of authority may be unable to anticipate what financial crisis the future may bring. As John Maynard Keynes, addressing the economic and financial future, put it so clearly in 1937:

"Our knowledge of the future is fluctuating, vague, and uncertain. . . . About these matters there is no scientific basis on which to form any calculable probability whatever. We simply do not know." Our expectation of the future, therefore, he continued, "being based on so flimsy a foundation . . . is subject to sudden and violent changes. The practice of . . . certainty and security suddenly breaks down. New fears and hopes will, without warning, take charge of human conduct."[13]

The year 2020 brought such "sudden and violent changes," to be sure. "New fear" marked the first half of the year. People were afraid not only for their lives from the virus, but also for their money from the bust. "We will likely face the sharpest and fastest contraction in activity in U.S. history," wrote *Grant's Interest Rate*

Observer in April, also reporting a forecast that "America faces a deflationary slump more severe than the unfondly remembered episodes of 1973–75, 1981–82 and even 2008–09."[14]

In April 2020, U.S. unemployment frighteningly shot up to its highest level since 1940, far higher at 14.8 percent than its previous peaks of 8.2 percent in 1975, 10.8 percent in 1982, and 9.9 percent in 2009, all reflecting great recessions. Stock prices dropped by 26 percent in four days and by 36 percent in six weeks in "one of the most dramatic stock market crashes in history."[15] Gross domestic product plummeted by 9 percent in one quarter. Futures prices for crude oil temporarily became negative. Even the market for "risk-free" U.S. Treasury securities didn't work well. Financial actors rediscovered the permanent truth that asset prices are ephemeral and can go down more than you thought—a lot more. We discuss in detail the numerous travails and fears of this time in Chapter 2, "The Panic of 2020."

The *Wall Street Journal* of April 4, 2020, proclaimed that March was "THE MONTH THAT CHANGED EVERYTHING," writing that "March began with a booming economy and ended with giant companies begging for bailouts." Not only giant companies, but everybody else, too, was begging for a government bailout. And the bailouts came—rightly, we judge, under the crisis circumstances—and were massive. One trader expressed the common experience: "I've never, ever, ever seen anything like this before."[16] A similar reaction: "I as an investor never thought that I would see a time in my life that was crazier than 2008. And here we are."[17]

In common with the last crisis, the governments and the central banks "had no choice but to fly by the seat of their pants, making it up as they went along."

The bailouts were consistent with the Cincinnatian Doctrine,[18] further discussed in Chapter 12, which suggests that periodic financial crises can only be addressed by the temporary expansion of the compact power, authority to command, and money printing ability of the government and its central bank—especially the money printing power, which shifts assets and risks to the government's balance sheet. These expansive, record interventions of 2020 are detailed in Chapter 3.

The second half of 2020 brought instead "new hopes." As additional surprises of 2020, a huge bull market in stocks, including highly speculative ones in cryptocurrencies and in houses, took off and continued in 2021. They accompanied a strong economic recovery. By June 2021, the *Wall Street Journal* could run on page 1 the headline, "U.S. Economy's Rebound Is 'Without Historical Parallel.'" This article quoted the distinguished economist, Allen Sinai, who has been in the economic forecasting business since 1971: "We've never had anything like it—a collapse and then a boom-like pickup. . . . It is without historical parallel."[19]

According to the Cincinnatian Doctrine, emergency interventions should always be temporary, to be turned off and unwound when normal times return, as they always, in time, do. In 2021, however, the interventions continued, although economic growth had resumed and people were benefitting from heroically developed vaccines against Covid. Financially, remarkable asset price inflation in high-priced bull markets, appropriately called the "Everything Bubble," continued. The price of one Bitcoin, which has no physical reality and represents no cash flow but does inspire interesting "new hope," peaked at over $63,000 in April 2021. It subsequently dropped about 50 percent, then went back up, doubling to a new high of over $67,000, fell again by about 48 percent, and demonstrates the extreme volatility of a speculative vehicle but remains surprisingly high. We consider the issues raised by cryptocurrencies in Chapter 6.

In addition to the asset price inflation, 2021 brought renewed rapid inflation in the prices of goods and services, with the rate of increase in the Consumer Price Index for 2021 accelerating to 7 percent. The Federal Reserve admitted it was surprised by the inflation, once again showing that central bankers' ability to forecast the economic and financial future, including the results of their own actions, is as poor as everybody else's. Compared to the actual inflation of 7 percent, the Federal Reserve in December 2020 had forecast 1.8 percent for 2021. A February 2021 survey of professional economic forecasters was almost as wrong as the central bank, with an average projection of 2.2 percent. The least wrong individual forecast was only 3.2 percent.[20]

At the same time, there was a continuing runaway inflation in the price of houses. The well-known Case-Shiller national house price index in December reported prices up over 19 percent. In January 2022, the AEI Housing Center reported that the house price inflation was continuing.[21] We consider the mortgage sector in Chapter 8.

With all this going on, the Federal Reserve's balance sheet nonetheless continued to bloat. In January 2022 it reached the truly remarkable sum of $8.9 trillion, more than double the $4.2 trillion of February 2020, reflecting the continuing life of the 2020 emergency programs. This was ten times the Federal Reserve's total assets in 2006. Not one of 2019's 30 official financial stability reports even faintly suggested there could be an $8.9 trillion Federal Reserve, nor did anybody else, including the Federal Reserve itself. Other central banks expanded correspondingly. As 2022 began, the Federal Reserve had belatedly announced it would "taper," or reduce its purchases of Treasury bonds and mortgage securities, and then stop increasing its portfolio by March. It had begun discussions of whether it might even reduce its mammoth size. We explore the role of central banks in Chapter 12.

Panic and extreme uncertainty marked the year 2020. The massive actions taken to survive the health-political-economic-financial crisis of that year continue in turn to create major uncertainty about what and how large their ongoing effects, and costs, will be. They will not be free. They already include the cost of the very high inflation of 2021 (unexpected, as noted, by the Federal Reserve's forecasts), which shrinks the value of savings and reduces real wages. How long the high inflation will go on is, as we write, hotly debated and unknown. This is a painful part of the fundamental, underlying uncertainty always there.

If we consider the history of various indexes that try to measure uncertainty, as reviewed for example in a 2020 Federal

Reserve study,[22] we find, as that paper says, "large uncertainty spikes, such as those appearing concurrently with the outbreak of Covid-19." It is true that the felt, or experienced, uncertainty suddenly soars at such times. But the real uncertainty of the future world was there before the uncertainty was so frighteningly felt. The real uncertainty was there the day before and in the months before the panic and always—people were simply not aware, or were only vaguely aware of it, perhaps even those who were diligently looking for the next crisis. And the crisis came—and we didn't see it coming.

Do the central bankers, and the rest of us, still "have trouble understanding what is happening," let alone what will happen? Of course. Every time. What the Roman poet, Claudian, wrote sixteen hundred years ago may be usefully applied to the economic and financial future of all times:

> *Res hominum tanta caligine volvi.*
> Human affairs are surrounded by so much fog.

As were the efforts at foresight of the authors, the FSOC, the central banks, and everybody else, when thinking about systemic risks in December 2019.

CHAPTER 2

The Panic of 2020

THE FIRST DEATH in the United States from the Covid virus was reported in February 2020. By March, there was financial panic, with plunges in asset prices and credit pressures not seen for more than a decade—not since the "Global Financial Crisis" of 2007–09. To rephrase T.S. Eliot, March was the cruelest month. The crisis manifested itself across virtually every sector of the U.S. economy, every part of the financial system, and around the world.

With the passage of time, now that we know how the recovery unfolded, it is already becoming difficult to remember how bad it was at the time, how intense the uncertainty, how dizzying was the sense of collapsing market prices, and especially how opaque the future seemed. The U.S. stock market went into free fall, as shown in Graphs 2.1 and 2.2, with the Dow Jones Industrial Average plunging 37 percent, and the Nasdaq index 30 percent, in one month.

The "TED spread," or the difference between the interest rate on short-term eurodollar deposits and that on short-term Treasury bills, is a measure of how much fear or confidence there is in money markets. Money market fear shot up dramatically in the Covid panic, as Graph 2.3 shows.

Widespread apprehension of the looming financial unknowns caused the prices of bank stocks, in particular, to collapse, dropping 48 percent in the month—see Graph 2.4. The banking system more than doubled its quarterly provision for loan losses

GRAPH 2.1

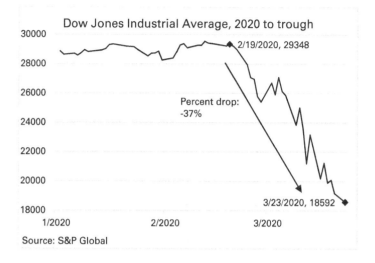

Dow Jones Industrial Average, 2020 to trough

2/19/2020, 29348

Percent drop: -37%

3/23/2020, 18592

Source: S&P Global

GRAPH 2.2

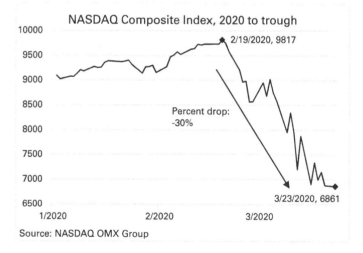

NASDAQ Composite Index, 2020 to trough

2/19/2020, 9817

Percent drop: -30%

3/23/2020, 6861

Source: NASDAQ OMX Group

during the rest of 2020—this provision averaged $125 billion per quarter for the second to fourth quarters of 2020.

As *always* happens in financial crises, as people and institutions faced intense financial uncertainty, a flight to cash, this time often called a "dash to cash," occurred. This is the same behav-

GRAPH 2.3

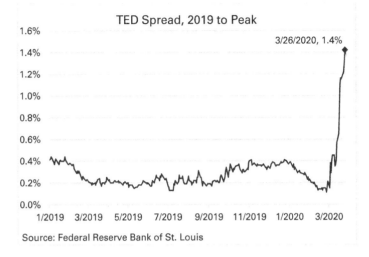

TED Spread, 2019 to Peak

Source: Federal Reserve Bank of St. Louis

GRAPH 2.4

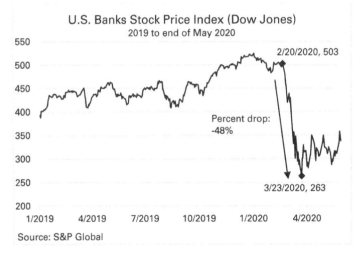

U.S. Banks Stock Price Index (Dow Jones)
2019 to end of May 2020

Source: S&P Global

ior described by classic economist David Ricardo (1772–1823) in his day as "a general panic," and by many others in similar terms since. However many computers we may own, and however sophisticated we think we are, this pattern doesn't change when widespread fear strikes.

Investors liquidated assets across all classes; sharp selloffs became the norm in virtually all markets, including the equity, short-term finding, corporate debt, and government debt markets; bid-ask spreads were quickly widening, there were demands for additional margin and increased rating downgrades across debt markets. In March, this flight to cash led to huge disruptions in the short- and long-term credit markets, a lack of investor demand for debt, a spike in interest rates, and a diminution of new debt issuance. By mid-March, panic even threatened in what was considered the world's most stable and liquid debt market—the market for U.S. Treasury securities, as huge selloffs led to illiquidity and disrupted the orderly functioning of even this market.

Nor did the panic spare the tax-advantaged municipal securities markets; investors sought liquidity by selling municipal bonds, resulting in falling prices, fewer bond issuances, and wide discounts from the net asset values of closed-end municipal bond funds.

The very large increases in bank loan loss reserves, shown in Graph 2.8 below, reflected growing risks and uncertainties in the credit of their borrowers, especially by increasing risks to the commercial real estate, energy, travel, and hospitality businesses. The flight to cash triggered large redemptions from prime money market and other types of mutual funds, which put strain on the asset management industry, as discussed further in Chapter 4.

Oil prices collapsed, and even became negative for a brief time in late April. You might think that should be impossible, but it happened in 2020, as shown in Graph 2.5. This made the peak-to-trough drop in the price of oil more than 100 percent.

Financial crises are always intertwined with economics and politics, but this one was something much more difficult to deal with: an intertwined health-political-economic-financial crisis, so the psychology of the panic added the fear of death to the fear of losing a lot of money. The beginning was entirely exogenous to the financial system: a mutated virus spreading from China that, however it developed, caused nationwide and worldwide fear, and fundamentally changed how Americans were living their lives

GRAPH 2.5

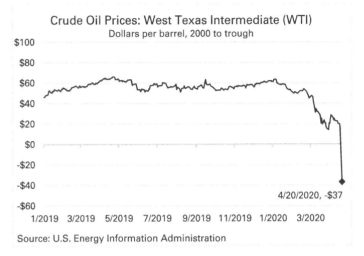

Crude Oil Prices: West Texas Intermediate (WTI)
Dollars per barrel, 2000 to trough

Source: U.S. Energy Information Administration

as they tried to cope with a new and ubiquitous threat of illness and death. In 2020, about 350 thousand Americans died of Covid infections. This was 0.1 percent of the population.

To limit the spread of the virus, governments shut down large portions of the economy, causing massive economic and social disruptions, putting millions of people out of work and thousands of organizations out of business. Without this government action, the death toll would presumably have been far worse, but the controls imposed by governments had huge economic and financial costs. They resulted in a severe economic contraction with enormous impacts on all aspects of American life. U.S. GDP fell over 9 percent from the first to the second quarter of 2020, as shown in Graph 2.6.

This was a crisis indeed. The GDP contraction was furthermore misleadingly popularized as a fear-inducing drop of over 30 percent, which is the number that results if the second quarter change is annualized—that is, if the quarter had gone on for a year, which it didn't. But it was bad enough in any case. In the end, GDP for the year 2020 as a whole fell 3.5 percent. This was much worse than in the "Great Recession" year of 2009, when U.S. GDP fell 2.5 percent.

GRAPH 2.6

U.S. Real GDP Change from Prior Quarter
Not Annualized (percent)

Source: BEA

This economic contraction was mirrored in other countries, with an aggregate 12 percent quarterly GDP drop for the second quarter of 2020 in the "G-7" major economies. The GDPs of the 36 countries of the Organization for Economic Co-operation and Development (OECD) in total contracted by 9.8 percent in that quarter: "an unprecedented fall . . . the largest drop ever recorded for the OECD area," the OECD reported.[1]

No one knew how it would all turn out; optimistic and pessimistic predictions competed, as always. It was once again demonstrated that economics is not a science. There were hyperbolic levels of perceived risk and uncertainty around the world and for virtually every American and the American economy, financial system, and society as a whole.

Beginning in February 2020, the government-mandated lockdowns led to a record level of unemployment, with the U.S. unemployment rate peaking at almost 15 percent in April 2020. This was far higher than during the "Great Recession" of 2007–09, far higher than the unemployment peaks during the steep recessions of 1975 and 1982, and indeed was by far the highest unemployment rate of the entire post-World War II era. This is vividly shown in Graph 2.7.

GRAPH 2.7

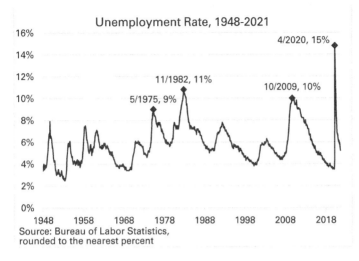

Unemployment Rate, 1948-2021

4/2020, 15%

11/1982, 11%

10/2009, 10%

5/1975, 9%

Source: Bureau of Labor Statistics,
rounded to the nearest percent

People who were unemployed might become unable to meet their credit obligations, such as credit card debt, student loans, consumer loans, mortgage debt, and rental payments. The government crisis response was to mandate widespread moratoria on foreclosures and evictions and require forbearance on loan payments. By government fiat, loans with borrowers behind on their payments because of the pandemic could not be classified as delinquent, even though the borrowers were not paying.

The negative impact of unemployment on household income, coupled with the granting of mortgage and rent forbearances, put significant stress on the housing finance industry. The independent mortgage companies that are not part of banking companies, and are therefore not protected by backup from the Federal Reserve and deposit insurance, are dependent on selling their loans to Fannie Mae and Freddie Mac and on Ginnie Mae securitizations. These non-bank mortgage companies increasingly dominate the servicing of U.S. residential mortgage loans, which constitute a huge loan market of about $11 trillion. Mortgage servicing companies are bound contractually to advance payments to mortgage-backed securities investors even if the servicers do not receive the corresponding payments from the mortgage borrowers. This obligation appeared to threaten their solvency.

Simultaneously, the inability of people to travel and gather in groups led to disruptions in the travel, hotel, retail, energy, movie, and restaurant industries, and for the lenders who financed these industries.

To summarize, by April 2020, widespread lockdowns had driven the seasonally adjusted U.S. unemployment rate to 14.8 percent, a frightening increase over the 3.5 percent of February, only two months before. U.S. GDP plunged from an annualized $21.5 trillion in the first quarter of 2020 to $19.5 trillion in the second. A huge selloff in equities drove the stock market down, led by massive declines in the market sectors most affected by the pandemic, including air carriers, cruise lines, and energy producers. The money markets and debt markets were panicked.

In the midst of all this, as noted above, even the market for U.S. Treasury securities did not escape the turmoil. It is impossible to overemphasize the importance of this market, not only for U.S. and global financial markets, but for the security and political functioning of the United States itself.

Treasury securities provide the debt funding needed for the vast operations of the U.S. government. Since these securities are backed by the full faith, credit, and power of the government of the United States and the money printing power of the Federal Reserve, which is part of that government, they are typically deemed to be risk-free—although nothing is truly risk-free, as the crisis demonstrated.

Treasuries serve as a world-wide benchmark for other securities, finance American military power, are used by the Federal Reserve to implement monetary policy, and are used extensively by financial actors for investments and hedging. Sovereign governments, central banks, and financial institutions hold and trade large portfolios of Treasury securities. It is not an exaggeration to say that the smooth functioning of the Treasury market is essential to the workings of U.S. and global financial markets, underpins the dollar as the world's reserve currency, and supports U.S. political and military power.

But in March 2020, the functioning of the Treasury market was anything but smooth. Holders of Treasuries seeking cash executed massive sales of Treasury securities, which resulted in increased volatility, unexpectedly reduced liquidity, a widening of bid-ask spreads, and an inability of market makers to efficiently handle trades.

This problem resulted, first and foremost, from the "dash to dollar cash" by many large holders of Treasuries, including foreign investors and central banks. These sales mostly occurred in off-the-run Treasury securities, which trade less frequently than the most recently issued ("on the run") Treasury securities. Ordinarily, these securities would be purchased by market makers, such as bank-affiliated broker-dealers and principal trading firms. But dealers entered March of 2020 with very high Treasury inventory levels, which made it difficult for them to absorb these sales, particularly since some were reportedly hitting internal risk limits in both on-the-run and off-the-run Treasury securities.

The cumulative result of these factors was illiquidity in the world's most liquid market. The increased illiquidity of off-the-run Treasuries resulted in a widening price spread between on-the-run and off-the-run securities, in spite of the fact that they are essentially identical securities issued at different times, but with differences in how easily they are traded.

These conditions, caused by heavy sales of Treasuries by unleveraged or "real money" investors, were exacerbated by the unwinding of highly leveraged positions held by some hedge funds, which engaged in so-called "Treasury basis trades." These positions used high leverage to seek to profit from the relatively narrow price differences between Treasury securities in the cash market and Treasury futures contracts. In the pressures of the panic, the relative prices turned these positions into losers. When Treasury market liquidity was restored by Federal Reserve interventions, the Federal Reserve effectively bailed out the hedge funds involved in these trades. One might visualize this as a script for an episode of the television show *Billions*. Could the Federal Reserve have been happy about being forced to help the hedge funds caught in these losing Treasury basis trades? It is easy enough to say that a central bank should not bail out troubled speculators, but in a crisis, it does so anyway.

So, a reasonable question is: To what extent should very large, highly leveraged positions by private investors such as hedge funds be able to jeopardize the functioning of markets for Treasury securities in times of stress? In a November 2021 report, "Recent Disruptions and Potential Reforms in the U.S. Treasury Market: A Staff Progress Report," the Treasury, Federal Reserve, Securities and Exchange Commission, and Commodities Futures Trading Commission proposed principles for the Treasury market. They notably suggest that "leverage that makes the financial system vulnerable to instability should be avoided."[2] We believe that constraining leverage in the Treasury market through some appropriate form of margin requirements would be consistent with the verity that "Leverage is the Snake in the financial Garden of Eden," as 2020 demonstrated yet once again.

The 2020 disruptions in the Treasury market were repeated in other short-term wholesale funding markets, both in the markets for secured transactions like repurchase agreements and securities lending, and for unsecured markets like commercial paper. The short-term wholesale funding markets total about $10 trillion, are critical providers of short-term funds to corporations, financial institutions, and governments, and are a crucial part of the daily operation of the financial system.

Repurchase agreements ("repos") allow participants to borrow funds that are secured by marketable securities, usually Treasuries and government agency-guaranteed mortgage-backed securities. Technically, the borrower sells those securities with an agreement to repurchase them at a future date at a higher price, and the difference between the sale and purchase prices is effectively the interest paid by the borrower. These transactions are functionally equivalent to secured loans but, because they are treated as purchases and sales for some regulatory purposes, have legal advantages for the lender who "purchases" the securities and the borrower who "sells" them.

As an interesting historical perspective, repurchase agreements were originally the creation of clever lawyers seeking to avoid tax and regulatory provisions applicable to secured loans. They are a classic example of the elevation of form over substance. First used in 1917 by the Federal Reserve as a way of avoiding taxes on loan interest, repurchase agreements were also utilized by banks as a way of avoiding borrowing and lending restrictions. Since these transactions were formally structured as the sale and resale of securities rather than as secured loans, with the buy-in of tax and regulatory authorities, they were not reported as loans. Now this market has taken on a life of its own. Indeed, repurchase agreements are statutorily recognized as protected contracts under the Bankruptcy Code so that if the "borrower," or initial seller, in a repo goes bankrupt before the purchaser resells the securities back to it, the contract is still given effect—there is no automatic stay and the trustee in bankruptcy cannot avoid paying back in full as the second part of the transaction. Economically equivalent transactions structured as secured loans are treated differently in bankruptcy.

Many financial businesses that do not have access to deposits as a short-term funding source, including broker-dealers and mortgage real estate investment trusts (REITs), depend on the repo markets for a large portion of their short-term funding. The Federal Reserve is a major participant in the repo market, trading in U.S. Treasuries using repos. In March 2020, repo rates increased dramatically, reflecting the flight to cash as the securities that serve as repo collateral sold off, and as the price of the collateral fell, margin requirements on repos increased.

The market for commercial paper was also rocked by the Covid panic. Commercial paper consists of short-term notes that both financial and nonfinancial corporations use to fund their operations. Along with bank lines of credit, commercial paper often constitutes a principal source of short-term funding and liquidity. Interest rates on commercial paper spiked, and there was also a significant drop in the amount of commercial paper purchased, as shown in Graph 4.3 in Chapter 4.

These disruptions in the short-term wholesale credit markets were exacerbated by runs on prime money market funds that invest in short-term debt instruments, including commercial paper. In the two panicked weeks between March 11 and 24, net redemptions from publicly offered institutional prime funds totaled 30 percent of the funds' assets. This was even worse than in the September 2008 panic, when outflows over the worst two-week period were 26 percent.[3]

This classic bank-type run resulted in a major market for short-term debt drying up, further causing rates to spike and driving down demand for short-term debt instruments, particularly commercial paper. In Chapter 4, we examine how structural issues in prime money market mutual funds, and other funds that hold private debt, make runs on these funds likely in a crisis.

In the short-term municipal debt markets, panicked selling caused rates to spike there, too. In mid-March, for example, the Securities Industry and Financial Markets Association Municipal Swap Index yield jumped by 3.9 percentage points over the prior week, to 5.2 percent.[4] This stress was increased by inordinately large redemptions from tax-exempt money market funds, as their investors, too, sought safety in cash, as opposed to their usual confidence in near-cash assets.

At the beginning of 2020, corporate debt was at extremely high levels. Indeed, the corporate debt to GDP ratio was at the highest level ever. With the panic in March, new issuance of both investment grade and high-yield corporate bonds virtually ceased, and spreads in both markets increased dramatically. The dollar amount of high-yield bonds issued in March 2020 declined 86 percent to $4.2 billion from the $30 billion issued in February.[5] Increases in corporate debt downgrades by the credit rating agencies reflected *and* increased the perceived risk of the debt markets. By May 2020, the rolling three-month ratio of nonfinancial corporate downgrades to upgrades reached the highest level ever recorded led by so-called "fallen angels"—issuers downgraded from investment grade to high yield. The number of fallen angels went to its highest ever level since Lucifer and his cohorts were cast from Heaven.

These losses also hit the collateralized loan obligation (CLO) market. CLOs are a major purchaser of leveraged corporate loans, which they divide into senior and junior tranches, the junior tranches taking the losses first if the underlying loans default. By June 2020, over 20 percent of CLOs were failing overcollateralization tests on their junior tranches.

Municipal finances were severely threatened by the pandemic. Tax revenues fell, and revenues from various projects built with municipal bond debt, such as airports, stadiums, and office complexes were evaporating as the pandemic kept those facilities empty. At the same time, many municipal expenses were increasing, including those for education, as new school ventilation systems and increased space for social distancing were required, and health care, with hospital systems under great strain from the pandemic. Credit rating agencies saw the risk of municipal bond defaults from projects where revenue streams would be cut by the public's staying home, and bonds financing these types of projects were downgraded.

The flight to cash squeezed the municipal bond markets, which experienced withdrawals of $45 billion from municipal bond funds between March and April 2020. Municipal bond prices fell and issuers postponed new bond issuance. In April, the Federal Reserve launched its unprecedented Municipal Liquidity Fund facility to purchase debt from eligible state and local issuers.

Not surprisingly, during the Covid crisis the number of defaults and bankruptcies on high-yield bonds rose sharply. The trailing four-quarter U.S. high-yield default rate rose to 8.5 percent in the third quarter of 2020 from 3.4 percent in the prior year.[6] Defaults across the totality of U.S. corporate bonds and syndicated loans were at $97 billion in the second quarter of 2020, the highest since 2009.[7]

The lifestyle disruptions caused by Covid decreased the value of much commercial real estate, although the impact varied depending on the type of commercial real estate involved. The most negatively affected were the lodging and retail portions of the sector, as people were forced to stay home and to stay away from hotels and stores by lockdowns. The impact on office buildings was also negative, as offices were mostly empty, although leases were still in force. Properties such as warehouses, on the other hand, held up quite well, as online sales increased from people at home, and raised the need for these facilities.

Commercial real estate has always been one of the most highly leveraged portions of the economy, with $4.7 trillion of associated debt as of the second quarter of 2020,[8] and has been a frequent culprit in financial crises. The prices of commercial real estate can fall dramatically, wiping out what seemed at the time of the loan to be a safe collateral margin. For example, one shopping mall defaulting in 2020 was originally appraised at $195 million to support a loan of $100 million, but the 2020 re-appraisal was $61 million, a drop in estimated value of 69 percent. Another 2020 defaulting mall, originally appraised at $322 million to support a loan of $178 million, was appraised at $130 million after default, a drop of 60 percent.[9] Every financial crisis demonstrates that the answer to the question, "How much can asset prices fall?" is "More than you thought."

Banks fund roughly half of outstanding commercial mortgages. Small and mid-sized regional banks hold more than one-half of the bank-held commercial real estate loans, and community banks have disproportionately large real estate exposures. The outlook for commercial real estate continues to be uncertain because the pandemic may have caused long-lasting changes in people's behavior that will affect the economics of portions of the sector. Losses among lenders to the sector tend to lag behind the financial crisis. During the crisis, many of those who could worked from home, and many are still doing so as we write. Many companies are sharply cutting back their demand for office space and trying to sublet existing offices to somebody else. This has led to predictions that the shrinkage in demand for commercial office space will be long-lasting and to questions about what effect this will have on the commercial real estate market and its lenders as some building owners become unable to service their debt due to these shifts. For the consequent losses to work through the system takes time. Less demand for space leads to space being dumped on the market for sublease. As old leases expire, vacancies and reduced rents ensue, leading to defaults on commercial mortgages.

As 2021 ended, some businesses were planning on a return to the office, although the spread of the Omicron variant put this again in doubt, and others seemed prepared to accept working from home as a permanent model. Will the shift to working from home caused by the pandemic be temporary, or is the commercial office market facing a long-term contraction caused by a fundamental shift in the manner in which Americans behave? You will know more, Informed Reader, about how this issue has developed than we can know in early 2022.

Residential real estate showed weakness during the February-May 2020 period, as lockdowns and slowdowns in economic activity disrupted home construction and traditionally in-person events like home showings, appraisals, and closings. Annualized existing home sales fell from 5.8 million sales in February 2020 to 3.9 million in May.[10] Mortgage interest rates remained very low, at the unprecedented level of approximately 3 percent for 30-year fixed rate loans throughout 2020 and 2021. This reflected Federal Reserve holdings of mortgage securities, which grew to $2.6 trillion, bought at a pace of about $480 billion a year. In the wake of the Covid pandemic, these purchases stoked the nationwide house price bubble. The Federal Reserve announced in December 2021 that it would reduce the amount of its mortgage and bond purchases ("taper" them, in Fedspeak) at a rate that would result in these purchases ceasing in March 2022, but that meant it would buy additional mortgages in the intervening months. In general, the Federal Reserve is unsure of what to do about this systemically risky financial Frankenstein it has created. Here again, Informed Reader, you will know more than we can about what happened next.

During the pandemic, government actions led to an increased rate of residential mortgage delinquencies. The government provided numerous subsidies and accommodations, mandated forbearance by lenders, supplemented household income, and suspended foreclosures and evictions. For example, the Coronavirus Aid, Relief, and Economic Security Act (the CARES Act) allowed borrowers who had a federally backed mortgage, which is the majority of mortgages, to obtain mortgage payment forbearance. It mandated that loans that were current before a borrower began forbearance must continue to be reported as current, even though the borrower made no payments. The resulting delinquency statistics were obviously and intentionally incomplete. The forbearance rate peaked at 7.2 percent of outstanding residential mortgages in May 2020, but had fallen to 1.7 percent by November 2021.[11]

For a final accounting, the forbearance will have to end and the dust settle. As long as house prices stay high, foreclosures and losses can be avoided by simply selling the house at the new, higher price to the next "greater fool." How long will house prices stay so inflated, especially if interest rates return to normal, higher levels? That *is* the question as far as housing finance goes. We take it up again in Chapter 8.

Banks entered the Covid crisis with increased required capital and liquidity levels, imposed after the 2007–09 crisis, which helped the banking industry weather the 2020 crisis. Without all the government interventions and the flood of liquidity from the central bank, however, the banks would have suffered much more than they did. As it was, bank stock prices plummeted, as we have shown in Graph 2.4. Considering potential loan defaults, the banking system's provisions for loan losses spiked by 118 percent or $62 billion to $115 billion in the second quarter of 2020. They went on up from there, reaching $132 billion in the fourth quarter, which was 150 percent above the first quarter guess at future credit losses. This is shown in Graph 2.8. How bad would loan losses be? Of course, during the crisis, nobody knew.

Try to recreate vividly in your memory, Thoughtful Reader,

GRAPH 2.8

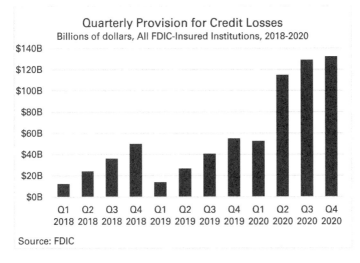

Quarterly Provision for Credit Losses
Billions of dollars, All FDIC-Insured Institutions, 2018-2020

Source: FDIC

the financial panic at the worst point of the 2020 crisis, March-April of 2020, and how frightening and utterly uncertain everything was. Unfortunately, these memories fade as time passes, and then, as new generations of financial managers and speculators arrive, the scene is set for the next crisis.

In Chapter 3, we consider the truly remarkable steps the federal government and the Federal Reserve took to prop up the financial system in the global panic and to finance the severe Covid economic contraction. However necessary, these steps involved enormous costs in the expansion of money printing, the explosion of government debt, and resulting dramatic inflation. During the panic, government actors properly worried first about the survival of the system, and their actions were successful in averting financial catastrophe. But the Covid crisis lives on in the effects of the steps taken to survive it. As we write, how these effects will ultimately turn out is still unknown, but we are experiencing unacceptably high consumer price inflation as one of the costs.

CHAPTER 3

Elastic Currency to the Rescue

WALTER BAGEHOT, a successful nineteenth-century English banker and the brilliant editor of *The Economist*, was a foundational thinker in the theory of central banking. He is well known to students of financial systems for his rule for central bank action in a financial crisis, which has been stated as follows: "To avert panic, central banks should lend early and freely (i.e., without limit), to solvent firms, against good collateral, and at high rates."[1] This is the classic guide for curing a panic in process, like the one in full bloom in March 2020.

In a truly remarkable and memorable series of emergency actions in the spring of 2020, the Congress, the Trump administration, the U.S. Treasury, and the Federal Reserve fully and wholeheartedly embraced Bagehot's prescription to lend freely. They embarked on massive lending programs to shore up many panicked financial market sectors and simultaneously to finance the Covid economic implosion with government debt and newly printed money. This dramatically expanded the money supply, government debt, and the Federal Reserve's balance sheet.

In a financial crisis, the flight to cash forces many leveraged financial entities, all at the same time, to try to reduce their risk and their balance sheets. Consider this question, Reflective Reader: Is it possible for all balance sheets to liquify into cash at the same time? An asset sold from one balance sheet must go to another one. Imagine that the entire financial system is one big balance sheet: How can the whole thing move into cash? The answer is that it can't, at least not without an utter collapse of asset prices, widespread debt deflation, and contagious insolvencies. For private balance sheets all to reduce risk together, while avoiding the implosion of a debt deflation, some other balance sheet must expand its loans, investments, and risk. That is what happened to the balance sheet of the government, and of its central bank in particular, beginning in the spring of 2020.

You may think of this as a great financial yin and yang, with private balance sheets fleeing risk in a panic and the central bank balance sheet correspondingly expanding, which is what we observe. That is why the Federal Reserve's balance sheet in reaction to the crisis of 2007–09 ballooned from $870 billion to $4 trillion, then in response to the 2020 crisis expanded from $4 trillion to over $8 trillion. As we write, the Federal Reserve's total assets are $8.9 trillion. We take this up further in Chapter 12.

When central banks lend, they can create new currency, thereby expanding the amount of money in existence. Monetary thinkers of a century ago called a currency that expands and contracts with the needs of the economy an "elastic currency." They set up the Federal Reserve System to provide it. As the Federal Reserve Act of 1913 explained in its first two lines, it is: "An Act To provide for the establishment of Federal reserve banks, *to furnish an elastic currency. . . .*"

The Federal Reserve furnished an elastic currency with a vengeance in 2020, and its program did work to end the financial panic, as Bagehot predicted. It was effective in restoring the smooth functioning of, and public confidence in, U.S. financial markets. The short-term effects of the federal programs were beneficial; the longer-term financial impact raises profound concerns.

The CARES Act, which provided over $2 trillion to subsidize businesses and households to support the economy through the Covid crisis, was rapidly passed and signed into law as an emergency measure on March 27, 2020. The CARES Act supported households through direct cash payments, expanded unemployment benefits, various forms of tax relief, forbearances for borrowers, and eviction and foreclosure moratoria for renters and homeowners. It provided cash to businesses, notably through the Paycheck Protection Program (PPP), which was a loan program aimed at small businesses and designed to encourage them to keep employees on their payrolls. The PPP loans could be and were forgiven and thus converted into government grants. The CARES Act also provided funding for state and local governments and health care providers, and subsidies for the airline industry and other businesses deemed critical for national security. It provided $454 billion to the United States Treasury to take the credit risk of various emergency facilities established by the Federal Reserve. It provided regulatory relief for financial institutions to reduce the pressures of the panic. It was huge, bipartisan, and it was necessary to avert an even worse contraction than the one already under way. These emergency actions to finance the bust and thereby to shorten it are listed in Table 3.1.

All of these programs accelerated a giant government deficit, as shown in Graph 3.2.

TABLE 3.1

Department of Treasury Emergency Programs
in 2020 and 2021

Tax credits for required paid leave by small and midsize businesses
Economic Impact Payments
Unemployment Compensation
Child Tax Credit expansion
Employee Retention Credit
Paid Leave Credit
Emergency Capital Investment Program
Paycheck Protection Program
State & Local Fiscal Recovery Fund
Capital Projects Fund
Homeowner Assistance Fund
Emergency Rental Assistance Program
Emergency Rental Assistance Program extension
State Small Business Credit Initiative
Coronavirus Relief Fund
Payroll Support Program
Payroll Support Program extension
Payroll Support Program further extension
Airline National Security Relief Loan Program
Coronavirus Economic Relief for Transportation Services Program
Employee Retention Credit
Payroll Tax Deferral

GRAPH 3.2

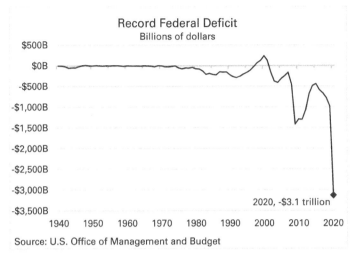

The deficit had to be financed with government debt, which the Federal Reserve committed to buy without limit during the panic and continued to buy at a rate of $1 trillion a year up to December 2021. Although it is little understood, the real first mandate of all central banks is to lend money to the government of which they are a part, as needed, which was forcefully demonstrated by the Federal Reserve in 2020–21. The result was an over $4 trillion, or about 100 percent, expansion of the Federal Reserve balance sheet, as shown in Graph 3.3. The effect of this inflationary expansion is already apparent in the high inflation of 2021 and early 2022; it will have further results still obscured by the fog of the future.

The Federal Reserve took rapid and radical actions to support financial markets, asset prices, and the economy, when confronted by the panic of 2020. On March 5 and again on March 15, it lowered short-term interest rates almost to zero. It significantly expanded its repurchase agreement operations to shore up weaknesses in the repo markets. It eased bank capital, liquidity buffers, and reserve requirements, encouraged banks to borrow from the discount window, and extended the period for these borrow-

GRAPH 3.3

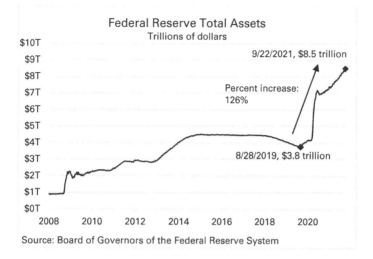

Source: Board of Governors of the Federal Reserve System

ings. As central bank to the world for U.S. dollar financing, the Federal Reserve increased the ability of foreign central banks to borrow dollars through U.S. dollar "swap line" arrangements with these other central banks. It created a repo facility for foreign central banks to borrow dollars by pledging U.S. Treasury securities rather than having to sell those securities, thus reducing the selling pressure on U.S. Treasury markets.[2]

The Federal Reserve reestablished emergency credit facilities originally put in place during the 2007–09 crisis and set up numerous new ones. Some of these were pursuant to authority in the CARES Act; others were set up under the emergency authority of Section 13(3) of the Federal Reserve Act, which required and promptly got the approval of the Secretary of the Treasury. Close cooperation between the Treasury and the Federal Reserve marked the entire crisis, as it did the 2007–09 crisis, and has continued, displaying the accuracy of the 1950s saying that the Federal Reserve is "independent within the government." The announcements of the emergency facilities, even before they began operating, immediately improved confidence and reduced fear in the roiled financial markets.

A number of these emergency programs focused on stabilizing short-term funding markets. They included:

The **Commercial Paper Funding Facility** to fund the issuance of commercial paper, a market under severe stress.

The **Primary Dealer Credit Facility**, which enabled the Federal Reserve Bank of New York to make secured loans to primary dealers, the institutions designated to trade with the U.S. government to implement Treasury debt issuance.

The **Money Market Mutual Fund Liquidity Facility**, to finance withdrawals from money market funds by permitting the Federal Reserve Bank of Boston to lend funds to financial institutions to purchase assets from these funds.

The **Municipal Liquidity Facility**, which authorized the Federal Reserve, with the credit loss risk taken by the U.S. Treasury, to purchase up to $500 billion of short-term debt issued by state and local governments. Only the State of Illinois and the New York Metropolitan Transportation Authority, two of the weakest credits in the municipal debt markets, borrowed under this facility.

Other lending facilities provided credit to businesses and households, including:

The **Paycheck Protection Program Liquidity Facility**, which permitted the Federal Reserve Banks to lend to financial institutions participating in the PPP, to fund PPP loans to small businesses.

The **Term Asset-Backed Securities Loan Facility**, originally part of the 2007–09 crisis bailout, which financed asset-backed securities backed by secured loans like auto loans and credit card loans.

The **Primary Market Corporate Credit Facility** and the **Secondary Market Corporate Credit Facility** set up to purchase, respectively, new and existing corporate debt.

The **Main Street Lending Program**, to fund loans to small and medium-sized businesses.

Table 3.4 summarizes the 14 emergency lending programs invented and implemented by the Federal Reserve in coordination with the Treasury and their acronyms. These might be entitled "The Bagehot Memorial Lending Freely Programs."

The principal financing source for all the emergency programs was monetization of debt by the Federal Reserve; in simpler words, printing money. The money stock accordingly had a dramatic acceleration, as shown in Graph 3.5.

These massive government interventions had a powerful effect in stabilizing financial markets, not least by shifting the risks and uncertainty from the investors and lenders to the government and the taxpayers.

By June 2020, the TED spread (the difference between the interest rate on short-term eurodollar deposits and that on short-term Treasury bills) had returned to normal, as shown in Graph 3.6, reflecting the market's calmed concerns about credit risk.

Similarly, the interventions quickly normalized both the amount of commercial paper issued and interest rate spreads in the commercial paper and repurchase agreement markets, which began to stabilize in April.

TABLE 3.4
Federal Reserve Emergency Lending Programs in 2020

3/17/2020	Primary Dealer Credit Facility (PDCF)
3/17/2020	Commercial Paper Funding Facility (CPFF)
3/18/2020	Money Market Fund Liquidity Facility (MMLF)
3/22/2020	Term Asset-Backed Securities Loan Facility (TALF)
3/22/2020	Primary Market Corporate Credit Facility (PMCCF)
3/22/2020	Secondary Market Corporate Credit Facility (SMCCF)
3/31/2020	Foreign and International Monetary Authorities Repo Facility (FIMA)
4/8/2020	Municipal Liquidity Facility (MLF)
4/8/2020	Paycheck Protection Program Liquidity Facility (PPPLF)
4/8/2020	Main Street Expanded Loan Facility (MSELF)
4/8/2020	Main Street New Loan Facility (MSNLF)
4/30/2020	Main Street Priority Loan Facility (MSPLF)
7/16/2020	Nonprofit Organization Expanded Loan Facility (NOELF)
7/16/2020	Nonprofit Organization New Loan Facility (NONLF)

GRAPH 3.5

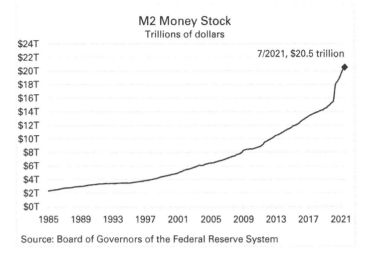

M2 Money Stock
Trillions of dollars

7/2021, $20.5 trillion

Source: Board of Governors of the Federal Reserve System

GRAPH 3.6

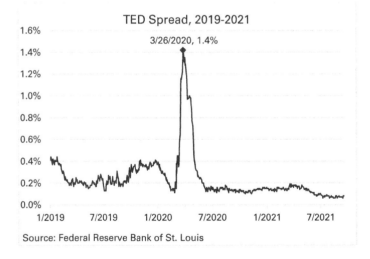

TED Spread, 2019-2021

3/26/2020, 1.4%

Source: Federal Reserve Bank of St. Louis

The emergency programs, together with the Federal Reserve's actions to lower short-term interest rates to close to zero and long-term rates to record lows, enabled borrowers to issue bonds at low yields. Issues of investment grade debt hit a record of $298 billion in April 2020. High yield or "junk bonds" also benefited from the

GRAPH 3.7

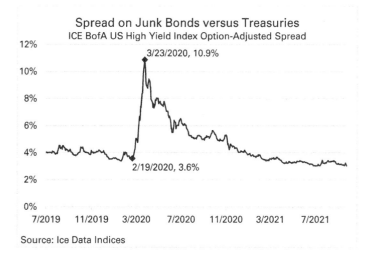

Spread on Junk Bonds versus Treasuries
ICE BofA US High Yield Index Option-Adjusted Spread

3/23/2020, 10.9%

2/19/2020, 3.6%

Source: Ice Data Indices

flood of government liquidity and low interest rates. The spread on junk bonds compared to Treasuries returned to its 2019 level by the end of 2020, as shown in Graph 3.7.

The emergency federal programs, together with Federal Reserve announcements in March that it would increase without any specific limit the size of its holding of U.S. Treasury securities, rapidly alleviated the turmoil in the Treasury securities market and the spike in the widening of bid-ask Treasury spreads.

Municipal debt issuance recovered from a low of $20.3 billion in March 2020 to $73.5 billion by October 2020.

Interestingly, personal bankruptcy filings were down in 2020. According to MarketWatch, there were 496,565 consumer bankruptcies in 2020, a 31-percent decline from 2019 and the lowest number since 1987.[3] The reduction in bankruptcies occurred because the government propped up income by expanding its own debt, and mandated the deferral of payments on mortgages, rents, and student loans. Thus, the government financed the bust and the crisis, but many loan payments still will ultimately have to be made. A notable political debate is whether this will include the huge amount of student loans which are delinquent in fact, if not always in official reports. We explore this failed government lending program in detail in Chapter 11.

The U.S. economy had recovered by the end of 2020, with GDP up to an annualized $22.7 trillion in the fourth quarter of 2020, which was 5 percent higher than the fourth quarter of 2019. The economic growth continued in 2021, which ended with real GDP up 5.5 percent.

Everybody speculated and debated during the 2020 crisis about whether the future economic path would be "V" or "U" or "L"-shaped, and of course nobody knew. With the panic controlled by the massive emergency use of elastic currency, the path turned out to be V-shaped after all, as the optimists had maintained, and as shown by Graph 3.8.

Crucially, the spectacular scientific achievement of rapidly developed Covid vaccines, their production, and mass inoculations removed the panicked fear and the economically destructive lockdowns of 2020. But the Covid virus and its variations are still with us and apparently will be with us as a continuing fact of human life.

GRAPH 3.8

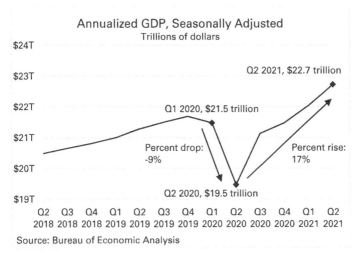

Annualized GDP, Seasonally Adjusted
Trillions of dollars

Q2 2021, $22.7 trillion

Q1 2020, $21.5 trillion

Percent drop: -9%

Percent rise: 17%

Q2 2020, $19.5 trillion

Source: Bureau of Economic Analysis

In 2020, aggressive expansion of elastic currency worked to stem the financial panic, as Bagehot said. But the effects of these actions are still unfolding in 2022, and as always, recurring financial crises will remain with us, also as a fact of human life.

CHAPTER 4

The Run on Prime Money Market Funds

MONEY MARKET FUNDS are an important financial sector, with, as we write, about $4.6 trillion in total assets in the U.S.[1] and worldwide assets, including the U.S., of about $7.6 trillion.[2] Although designed to be a very low-risk vehicle for holding risk-averse investments as a close money substitute, they can and do get in trouble in a financial crisis.

The panicked "dash to cash" in 2020 caused prime money market funds to experience very high and unexpected customer redemptions. As they tried to sell assets in order to raise the cash to honor redemptions, the markets became flooded with the debt instruments that the funds needed to sell but not enough other people wanted to buy. This, of course, pushed down the prices of those assets. The perceived risk of the funds increased, so more people demanded redemption of their investments in them, resulting in more selling and further destabilization of the short-term money markets.

This panicked downward spiral demonstrated a fundamental structural issue with these funds: the easy redemption they promise to investors depends on only a small percent of investors wanting out at any given time, just as is the case for the depositors of a bank. The problem is the same as the classic problem of a run on a bank or a run on the banking system.

Banks offer their depositors liquidity by promising to redeem their deposits in cash. As everybody knows, this works only as long as not too many people want their money back at once. If too many of them do, the bank can't keep its promise, and the game is over—unless somebody else bails out the bank. The same is true for money market funds. When push comes to shove, they all have a fundamental liquidity mismatch because they promise more liquidity to their holders than they have in their component assets. They simply do not have the ability to liquidate enough of their assets, which become increasingly illiquid in times of crisis, at high enough prices to accommodate large, simultaneous demands for withdrawals by their investors. This doesn't matter in ordinary times, when relatively few investors seek to withdraw funds and the markets for money market fund assets are stable, but it becomes a glaring vulnerability in a crisis, when a "dash to cash" always occurs. This is not an accident or a fluke, but a matter of money market funds' structural design—again just like banks.

The functioning of the financial system always depends on most people not demanding their money back. There is no more fundamental financial principle than this.

Money market funds try to and usually do maintain a stable net asset value of $1.00 per share, which means that investors come to expect redemption at that par price, just as you expect to redeem your bank account at par. If a fund is unable to redeem at par, it is called "breaking the buck." This imposes losses, although always small ones so far, on investors who firmly expected no losses at all. Breaking the buck is so contrary to investor expectations that it ruins confidence in the fund. Runs result when investors rush for the exit, but of course they cannot all exit at once.

"Money funds emerged as a flashpoint in March 2020," as the *Wall Street Journal* reported,[3] and it headlined a related commentary, "Money-Market Funds Buckled in Two Crises in a Row."[4] The two crises are 2008 and 2020. What can these funds do when their promise to redeem investments is called on by too many of their investors?

The problem is centered on prime money market funds, which invest in private money market instruments. The customers' demand for redemptions would ordinarily be met by the proceeds from maturing investments, drawing down existing bank accounts, or by selling the most marketable securities from their portfolio. Prime money market funds did these things in March of 2020, but it wasn't enough. So, some turned to the firms that sponsor them for financial support, and then ultimately turned to the Federal Reserve for help, becoming part of the story of the "elastic currency" discussed in Chapter 3. The Federal Reserve invented its Money Market Mutual Fund Liquidity Facility, which created money to lend to banks, so banks could purchase assets from money market funds, and the funds could give investors the cash they demanded. In the panic, the prime money market funds shrank, with their assets dropping 12 percent.

Government money market funds, whose only investments are government securities, are much larger than prime money market funds. In a crisis, when the universal cry is "Give me a government guarantee!" they have much more perceived safety. Indeed, the flight to cash might be more completely called "the flight to cash and Treasury bills." In the 2020 panic, the assets of the government money market funds rapidly increased, while the prime funds contracted, as shown in Graph 4.1.

GRAPH 4.1

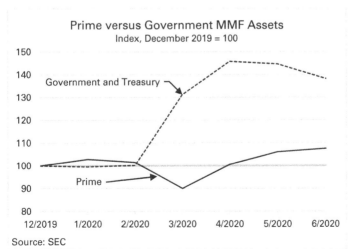

Prime versus Government MMF Assets
Index, December 2019 = 100

Source: SEC

Bond mutual funds also experienced customer redemption problems. These funds are typically invested in high-yield and investment-grade corporate debt. They experienced their heaviest redemptions since the last financial crisis in 2007–09. For them and for other bond investors, the Federal Reserve and the U.S. Treasury invented the Secondary Market Corporate Credit Facility. In this creative piece of financial engineering, the Federal Reserve committed to buy corporate bonds for its own balance sheet to prop up the market, and the Treasury took the primary risk of loss by putting taxpayers' money as equity into the Federal Reserve's special-purpose vehicle that bought the bonds.

The key temptation for both money market and bond funds is to try to increase their profits in normal times by promising their customers daily redemption of their funds—a promise they know in advance cannot always be kept, but most of the time seems a very low risk, since money market funds hold highly rated, short-term assets. These are easily saleable at predictable prices, until they are not, when these markets become illiquid during financial crises.

Prime money market mutual funds are major holders of commercial paper. In March 2020, the commercial paper market largely ceased to trade. So, when the funds most needed to sell their assets to meet redemption demands, they could not sell or could sell only by realizing losses. Money market funds' holding of commercial paper dropped by 25 percent in the first three quarters of 2020, as shown in Graph 4.2.

When the commercial paper market freezes up in this fashion, it creates an equally severe problem for the companies that rely on issuing this paper to fund themselves. In the 2020 panic and its aftermath, nonfinancial commercial paper outstanding dropped by 46 percent, as shown in Graph 4.3.

The liquidity mismatch is more pronounced for bond funds, which invest in longer-term, riskier assets that do not actively trade, but still promise daily redemption. Selling large amounts of debt instruments in stressed dealer markets is a process that takes time and effort. During this process, the prices of the assets up

GRAPH 4.2

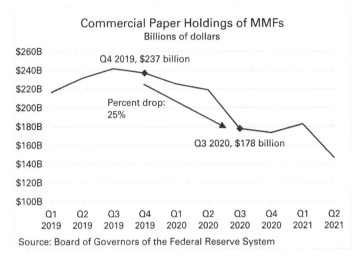

Commercial Paper Holdings of MMFs
Billions of dollars

Q4 2019, $237 billion

Percent drop:
25%

Q3 2020, $178 billion

Source: Board of Governors of the Federal Reserve System

GRAPH 4.3

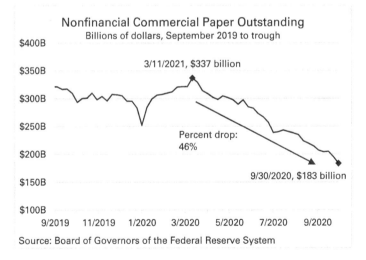

Nonfinancial Commercial Paper Outstanding
Billions of dollars, September 2019 to trough

3/11/2021, $337 billion

Percent drop:
46%

9/30/2020, $183 billion

Source: Board of Governors of the Federal Reserve System

for sale may move significantly against the entity under pressure to sell. Funds that offer customers daily redemptions at today's price, when it may take time to sell the assets at a falling price, may obviously experience liquidity problems.

These structural problems were already evident in the 2007–09 financial crisis, when the funds experienced similar redemption demands. By way of wider financial context, consider how banks historically solved this same fundamental illiquidity problem in the 1930s: by having the government guarantee their deposits with "deposit insurance." With the government guarantee, runs on banks became rare, and banks got to operate with less capital, but they also got extremely intrusive regulation in exchange. This banking solution also greatly expanded the moral hazard of the financial system, since it means most depositors don't have to care in the least if the bank they put their money in is sound, or even solvent.

For money market funds, however, the government response was different. In 2010, in the wake of the last crisis, the Securities and Exchange Commission implemented new regulatory requirements designed to control money market funds' risk of illiquidity. After amendments in 2014, the SEC required: that the average dollar-weighted maturity of investments held in a money market fund cannot exceed 60 days; that taxable funds must hold at least 10 percent of their assets in investments that can be converted into cash within one day; that at least 30 percent of their assets must be in investments that can be converted into cash within five business days; and that no more than five percent of assets can be held in investments that take more than a week to convert into cash. If a money market fund failed the 30 percent test, it could suspend redemptions temporarily and impose a liquidity fee on redemptions. If a fund failed to maintain at least ten percent of its assets in investments that can be converted into cash within five business days, it had to impose a liquidity fee on redemptions. The SEC also mandated a floating net asset value for prime funds marketed to institutional investors. In other words, these funds had to price redemptions at their net asset value rather than at a rounded price of $1.00 per share, while retail money market funds generally continued to be bought and redeemed at a buck a share.

It all sounded reasonable, but when the 2020 panic came along, it didn't work. Why not?

There were at least two big weaknesses in the SEC's attempted fixes.

The first is its 30 percent rule. In times of stress, such a bright line rule inevitably creates a "first mover advantage." If investors fear that a fund is at risk of failing the 30 percent test, or any other such regulatory gate, and that they may therefore be prohibited from redeeming or may have to pay a redemption fee, of course they try to be first to get their money out. They need to redeem quickly, before the others, to get their money out before the bright line is hit and redemptions are suspended or a fee imposed. In the 2020 crisis, prime fund redemptions accelerated in those funds whose percentage of assets approached the regulatory limits. The SEC's fixes appear to have perversely increased the risk they were designed to avoid. Moreover, if one fund limits redemptions, there is a risk that investors may withdraw from other funds for fear that they may restrict redemptions as well. Just as a run on one bank can trigger runs on other banks, the same is true for money market funds.

The second weakness is in the definition of "liquidity." We know that markets freeze up during a crisis and that liquidity disappears just when you need it, and indeed because you need it. A security that may be very liquid during normal times may become illiquid in a crisis. So, during a crisis, the previously liquid assets used to determine the SEC liquidity requirements may then be illiquid. Liquidity is not an inherent characteristic of an asset but fluctuates depending on the group behavior and group beliefs of financial actors at each particular point in time. Alas, Faithful Reader, as Alex has elsewhere explained, "Liquidity is a figure of speech."[5]

Following the panic of 2020, financial actors and regulators recognized the weaknesses of the previous reform efforts and looked for ways to reform the reforms. In the late days of the Trump administration, at the end of 2020, the President's Working Group on Financial Markets, a group chaired by the Secretary of the Treasury and including the Chairs of the Federal Reserve, the Securities and Exchange Commission (SEC), and the Commodities Futures Trading Commission (CFTC), released a report on the liquidity problems faced by money market funds in the Covid crisis.[6]

The President's Working Group Report explored a number of possible reforms, without endorsing any. The international Financial Stability Board published a policy paper in June 2021 that considered a very similar list of possibilities. These include the following ideas (not ranked by priority):

1. Removing the ties between money market fund liquidity and fee and gate thresholds—that is, removing the previous reform.
2. Reform of the detailed conditions for imposing redemption limits or fees.
3. Requiring a "minimum balance at risk," which means you can't take all your money out, but must leave some in the fund, with this portion perhaps subordinated to other investors.
4. Pricing the shares in the fund, and therefore redemptions, at floating net asset value for all prime and tax-exempt money market funds.
5. "Swing pricing" requirements, which means investors redeeming in times of stress are charged an extra fee theoretically equal to the liquidity cost created by their redemption.
6. Capital requirements for money market funds.
7. Requiring additional financial support from fund sponsors.
8. Creating a "Liquidity Exchange Bank" and requiring membership in it—a kind of special central bank for money market funds.[7]

These various proposals can be grouped as follows: Numbers 1 and 2 change the existing regulatory framework of liquidity gates and thresholds; 3, 4 and 5 seek to impose the cost of redemption solely on investors wanting to redeem; and 6, 7 and 8 seek to make clear to investors that there is liquidity risk and offer solutions to backstop redemptions.

On December 15, 2021, the SEC published the next chapter in this ongoing debate. Following up on the President's Working Group report, it produced a 325-page set of proposed amendments to its rules governing money market funds, including many of the proposals from the prior report,[8] such as raising the liquid asset requirement from a 10-percent daily reserve and a 30-percent weekly reserve to 25 percent and 50 percent, respectively. At the same time, they would eliminate the fees and gates structure imposed in 2014, their former reform. They would require money market funds to use market value in calculating their reserves, and mandate "swing pricing" for prime and tax-exempt money market funds, but not for government or retail money market funds. The SEC apparently rejected the ideas of a Liquidity Exchange Bank or imposition of sponsor support.

So, there are many proposals and the SEC has staked out a new position, but as we write, nothing has become final. Whatever the SEC finally adopts, we observe that, even with government deposit insurance and vast volumes of regulation, in recent decades the Federal Reserve and the Treasury have often been busy bailing out banks and savings and loan associations. Even with further reform, the Federal Reserve may find itself bailing out money market funds in a future financial crisis because of the size of this market, its impact on short-term funding markets and the financial system in general, and the fundamental economic disconnect between the promise to redeem everyone's shares upon demand and the inability to do so in a financial crisis—all ways that money market funds are like banks.

Unlike banks, money market mutual funds invest only in short-term assets such as government securities and short-term highly rated private debt, including commercial paper; like banks, they offer a usually safe rate of return. They offer daily redemption, unlike bank certificates of deposit, but like the directly competitive bank money market deposit accounts. Unlike bank deposits, they are not guaranteed by the federal government. Like the largest banks, they may benefit from the market perception that they would nonetheless be bailed out by the federal government, if necessary. Experience supports this perception, for the government has indeed intervened to preserve their value, finance the demand for redemptions, and prevent failures. The risk of these funds is low in normal times, but their liquidity risk rises in a financial crisis, a phenomenon that has been experienced in several countries. As the Financial Stability Board observed, "In both the 2008 and 2020 stress episodes, redemptions from money market funds did not abate until central banks and governments in several jurisdictions intervened."[9]

The timing and nature of future financial crises is unknowable, but all history suggests they will continue to occur. To protect against these recurrences, should the government guarantee all or some types of money market funds? We think the answer is No: it has too many guarantees piled up already. Or should the government promise never to make any future interventions, in order to force the market to price in all the risk? Who would believe that promise? We wouldn't. Would you, Candid Reader?

Among the proposed reforms, we do favor eliminating ties between money market fund liquidity and gate thresholds. Such bright line tests encourage first-mover redemption during a crisis, when such redemptions further destabilize markets and force sales of money market assets at depressed prices.

Another reform that makes sense is to require floating net asset values for retail as well as institutional prime money market funds, rather than a rounded share price of $1.00 per share. In this way, investors would better recognize the actual risk of their holdings. However, since crises always engender a flight to cash, the floating redemption price will not prevent the problems of illiquidity during the inevitable crises. As the Financial Stability Board also observed, "Variable net asset value funds can also experience large redemptions."[10]

Shining light on the real liquidity risk that money market funds face would likely make them less attractive to investors. The funds could reduce this risk by offering explicit sponsor support for redemptions, maintaining capital, having larger reserve buffers, or by arranging liquidity backstop lending lines with existing financial institutions. Of course, these actions would have costs, and funds with these features would have lower returns along with their lower risk. The SEC's proposal to require funds to hold more liquid assets in reserve would also reduce the profitability of those funds subject to the requirement. As we point out above, a critical problem with requiring a fund to increase its level of liquid assets is that assets that are "liquid" before a crisis may become illiquid during a crisis, just when their liquidity becomes most needed.

All this demonstrates that in the matter of promises of liquidity, as for all other financial risks, the fundamental economic law that "Nothing is free" applies. Every risk, in time, must be paid for by somebody.

CHAPTER 5

A Second Surprise
The Amazing 2020–21 Market Boom

IN THE WAKE of the 2020 financial panic, with historically unprecedented levels of government peacetime interventions and elastic currency to the max, even though the Covid health crisis and its uncertainty continued, an amazing financial market boom took off. First there was the financial crisis, then came "The Everything Bubble," as it has been called. Noted investor Jeremy Grantham called it "the most dangerous breadth of asset overpricing in financial history."[1] Equity prices, bond prices, house prices, and cryptocurrency prices all soared to previously unimaginable levels, with these prices boosted by exceptionally low interest rates which, it is said, are the lowest in 5,000 years. Real (inflation-adjusted) interest rates were negative and fueled the boom which continued on through 2021.

The Covid financial crisis was the First Big Surprise of 2020. The huge succeeding asset price boom was the Second Surprise.

Equity prices hit their 2020 panicked low point on March 23. A year later, the Dow Jones Industrial Index was up 76 percent; the S&P 500 Index had increased 76 percent, and the Nasdaq index had increased 100 percent. From the low to September 23, 2021, 18 months later, the respective price increases were 87 percent, 99 percent and 119 percent. The investors' panic and fear were gone, replaced by bull market enthusiasm.

During this period, house prices also rose dramatically, with the median existing-home sales price in May 2021 nearly 24 percent higher than it was in the preceding May. By June 2021, the Case-Shiller house price index was far over its previous Housing Bubble peak of 2006. From March 2020 to June 2021, this leading house price index rose 21 percent. Adjusted for inflation, it was up 15 percent. It certainly looks like a new housing bubble. Energy prices strongly recovered from their crisis collapse. The prices of Bitcoin and other cryptocurrencies went hyperbolic. This was both a fascinating and surprising sequence of events.

The 2020–21 path of asset prices skyward is shown dramatically by the equity market examples in Graphs 5.1 and 5.2, and the house prices in Graphs 5.3 and 5.4.

Essential to all of these remarkably elevated asset prices were extremely low interest rates, a result of the actions of the Federal Reserve and the other major central banks. On March 8, 2020, the key 10-year Treasury note yield hit a record low of 0.32 percent. Although the trading market in Treasuries was in turmoil, investors during the Covid panic sought safety above all by owning Treasuries. To paraphrase the classic words of Will Rogers, they stopped worrying about the return *on* their principal and instead worried about return *of* their principal.

GRAPH 5.1

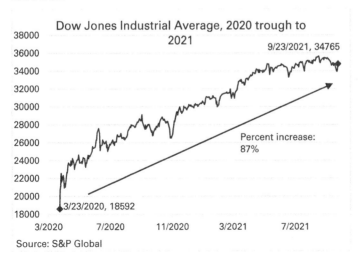

Dow Jones Industrial Average, 2020 trough to 2021

9/23/2021, 34765

Percent increase: 87%

3/23/2020, 18592

Source: S&P Global

GRAPH 5.2

NASDAQ Composite Index, 2020 trough to 2021

9/23/2021, 15052

Percent increase: 119%

3/23/2020, 6861

Source: NASDAQ OMX Group

GRAPH 5.3

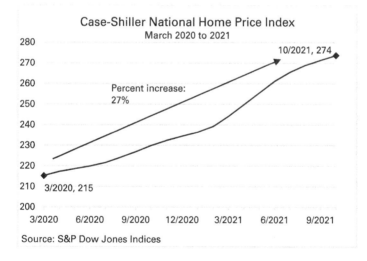

Case-Shiller National Home Price Index
March 2020 to 2021

10/2021, 274

Percent increase: 27%

3/2020, 215

Source: S&P Dow Jones Indices

At the end of September 2021, the 10-year Treasury yield was still exceptionally low at about 1.5 percent, far below its long-term historic levels, as shown in Graph 5.5. In January 2022, it rose to 1.8 percent, still extremely low compared to history.

GRAPH 5.4

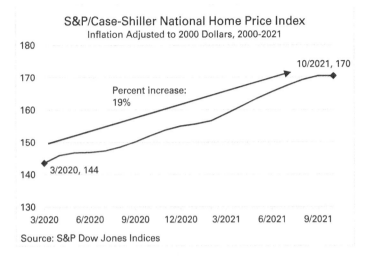

S&P/Case-Shiller National Home Price Index
Inflation Adjusted to 2000 Dollars, 2000-2021

Percent increase: 19%

10/2021, 170

3/2020, 144

Source: S&P Dow Jones Indices

GRAPH 5.5

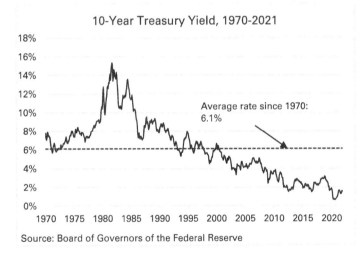

10-Year Treasury Yield, 1970-2021

Average rate since 1970: 6.1%

Source: Board of Governors of the Federal Reserve

Were these record low yields a "new normal" of everlasting low interest rates, or a transitory effect of the Covid crisis and unsustainable central bank bond-buying and money-printing? We believe it is the latter, and if that is so, large losses are in store for bondholders when interest rates return to something more normal. That would end the asset price inflation in bonds; then other asset prices, facing higher discount rates and lower present values of their cash flows, would follow. When will that be? Through the end of 2021, the great 2020–21 bull markets went on, but as we write in early 2022, Federal Reserve watchers are forecasting as many as four rate increases in 2022 to address the high inflation, and the Federal Reserve has announced it will stop its bond and mortgage buying in the spring. Equity markets sold off in January 2022 for their worst month since the Covid panic, reflecting the impact on market expectations of upcoming interest rate increases, with many speculative stocks taking especially large losses. There were significant withdrawals from municipal bond funds and the interest rates on residential mortgage loans went up. Was the long party at last petering out?

Graph 5.6 compares the rate of consumer price inflation to the yield on the 10-year Treasury note. As consumer price inflation spiked upwards in 2021 to 7 percent for the year, the holders of a 10-year Treasury note were losing 7 percent per year to inflation, while being paid interest of 1.7 percent or less. They were thus

GRAPH 5.6

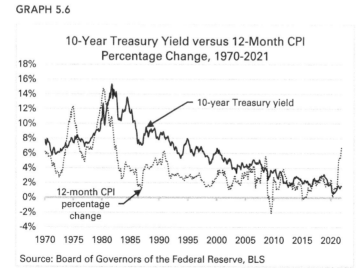

10-Year Treasury Yield versus 12-Month CPI Percentage Change, 1970-2021

Source: Board of Governors of the Federal Reserve, BLS

losing about four times as much in reduced purchasing power of their money as they were getting in interest. This is a classic fate of bondholders in an inflationary period.

Assuming that the Federal Reserve succeeds in its self-appointed goal of perpetual inflation—that is, always having 2 percent inflation instead of stable prices—the purchasing power lost in 2021 is gone forever, because even should the *rate* of inflation decline in the future, inflation will continue and the dollar's purchasing power will continue to fall. But future bond investors, other than the Federal Reserve, will presumably demand interest rates that cover the purchasing power lost to inflation. That would mean interest rates higher than the expected rate of inflation, in other words, positive real interest rates instead of negative ones. We believe that this must happen at some point, one way or another.

Graph 5.7 shows the 50-year history of the real interest rates on the 10-year Treasury note, defined as its yield minus the CPI inflation rate at each point. It shows that real 10-year Treasury rates have not been as negative as in 2021 since the Great Inflation days of 1980, forty years before. They will not remain that

GRAPH 5.7

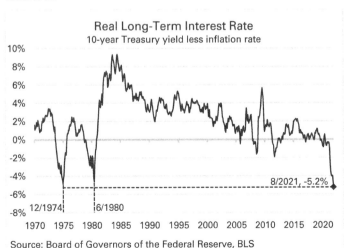

Real Long-Term Interest Rate
10-year Treasury yield less inflation rate

8/2021, -5.2%

12/1974   6/1980

Source: Board of Governors of the Federal Reserve, BLS

way. As we have discussed, the high inflation of 2021 was a big surprise to the Federal Reserve, whose inflation forecasts completely missed what actually happened as a result of their own actions. What will their next surprise be?

We have been considering bondholders. Let us turn to savers, who get a short-term interest rate on their savings that is substantially negative after inflation. As we write, the return on their savings is about negative 7 percent in real terms, as shown in Graph 5.8. Their savings are in fact being expropriated by the Federal Reserve, without legislation, to help finance the record government deficits, which in turn finance the government's responses to the Covid crisis. The pain of this government expropriation is disproportionally suffered by seniors and retirees who traditionally have sought to invest their laboriously acquired nest eggs in relatively safe, income-producing instruments like government bonds and bank certificates of deposit. At the same time, the negative real rates have generated large profits for investors in the Everything Bubble, especially if they are leveraged with cheap debt.

In many countries, both nominal and real interest rates were and are negative. A decade or more ago, negative nominal inter-

GRAPH 5.8

Source: Board of Governors of the Federal Reserve, BLS

est rates were believed by many economists to be impossible, because they thought that interest rates had a "zero lower bound." They don't, as it turned out. Now everybody knows there can be negative nominal interest rates, but nobody knows how negative they can become. One argument for central bank digital currencies, a possibility we take up in Chapter 6, is that governments can then make interest rates even more negative.

Thus, as we have seen, the aftermath of the Covid pandemic brought the U.S. a renewed, rapid economic expansion, and amazing bull markets in many investments. This was fueled by large government payments and subsidies, huge government deficits, a regime of essentially zero-percent short-term nominal interest rates, record low long-term interest rates, a vast monetization of both government debt and mortgages, and negative real interest rates. Inflation revived and grew hot, making real interest rates more negative. While these were continuing, President Biden sought a government budget that would result in $6.5 trillion in new government spending for a budget already in record deficit, although as we write, it appears that the largest part of this proposal will not be enacted.

As discussed, house prices soared even higher than at the top of the great Housing Bubble in 2006. In addition to reflecting the record low mortgage interest rates, the rapid increase in house prices has been attributed in part to people looking for more space and larger homes due to the lockdowns and other restrictions imposed by governments to control Covid. Those who have the ability to work remotely have been able to move and buy in less expensive and often less heavily taxed cities, which results in house prices being bid up there.

With the post-Covid boom in energy prices, oil prices soared back to $70 per barrel by September 2021, as shown in Graph 5.9. By October, they were over $80 per barrel and ended January 2022 at $88. Recall they had dropped to less than zero at their Covid crisis bottom. Similarly, the prices of natural gas and coal boomed. "An acute shortage of natural gas and coal supplies stemming from the gathering global economic recovery has

GRAPH 5.9

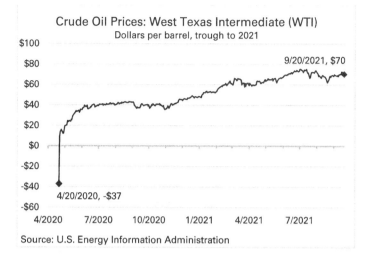

Crude Oil Prices: West Texas Intermediate (WTI)
Dollars per barrel, trough to 2021

Source: U.S. Energy Information Administration

sparked a precipitous run-up in prices for energy supplies," the
International Energy Agency reported in October 2021,[2] adding
in January 2022, "Exceptionally high gas—and by extension electricity—prices . . . are likely to have a lasting negative impact."[3]

In the post-Covid, Everything Bubble world, mini-bubbles
formed and corrected in a variety of highly speculative assets—
for example, the shares of GameStop, a retailer of video games. As
the story is told, in January 2021, after learning that several hedge
funds were shorting GameStop shares to bet that the shares
would decline, a group of speculative investors began buying the
stock, not because of any perception of underlying value, but to
cause the hedge funds to lose money and, through a classic short
squeeze, make the shares rise. They belonged to a populist Reddit
forum with an avowed aim to take on Wall Street, and their gam-
bit wildly succeeded. In January, GameStop shares went up from
a low of $17 per share to a high of $483. By February 22, the mini-
bubble had deflated and the price had fallen to $46 a share, down
90 percent from the peak. It recovered again and was $184 at the
end of October 2021, down 62 percent from its bubble peak, then
again fell to $109 by the end of January 2022. It was then down 77

percent from the peak but was still five times its price at the end of 2020.

What are we to make of such extreme volatility, apparently not based on any underlying fundamentals of the stock? Prices have no material or substantive reality, and asset prices can go both up and down a lot more than you may think possible.

A remarkable bubble also emerged in Bitcoin, a cryptocurrency not supported by any underlying asset or any cash flow. While GameStop, whatever its stock price may be, is a real company, the value of Bitcoin is completely based on perception. "Esse est percipi" ("To be is to be perceived"), the idealist philosopher, Bishop Berkeley famously postulated. The old metaphysician would have been delighted to see his principle come true with the development of Bitcoin and other cryptocurrencies.

Berkeley's postulate is reflected in the musings of one recent commentator, John Hussman, about financial markets: "If you think about markets, markets are basically places where people have beliefs, they turn them into behaviors, they produce market behavior, and then that market behavior comes back around and informs their beliefs."[4]

One of the great financial marketing coups was when Bitcoin convinced people to refer to what is only an electronic bookkeeping entry as a "coin." Now the media endlessly show pictures of gold coins with a "B" on them when discussing this purely intangible accounting entry. We take up the intriguing world of cryptocurrencies in detail in Chapter 6, which shows the remarkable Bitcoin price boom, price drops, and volatility in Graph 6.1.

This surge in asset prices across the board reflects the way the government flooded the markets with loans and subsidies through its CARES Act programs as well as with massive printing of new money by the Federal Reserve. U.S. government policy, while successfully bridging the Covid crisis, also fed the bubbles.

What next? Governments, central banks, and financial actors always imagine and hope for booms to end with a soft landing. But the larger and longer-lasting the bubble, the larger the potential damage when it shrivels in the inevitable bust. Everything you get must be paid for in some fashion. We can predict that the bust will come, but, as financial history demonstrates, we will not be able to predict accurately when it will happen, exactly what will precipitate it, or how bad it will be.

As you are considering this chapter, Future Reader, will the great 2020–21 Everything Bubble have already imploded as did its predecessors, perhaps when interest rates finally rose to normal levels, reacting to a severe inflation? Perhaps you already know the answer, which is still in the fog of the future for us.

CHAPTER 6

Cryptocurrencies

An Assault on Central Banks or Their New Triumph?

THE AMAZING BULL—or bubble—market in the price of Bitcoin and other cryptocurrencies was another surprise of late 2020 and of 2021. The price of a Bitcoin, for example, went virtually straight up from $10,000 in October 2020 to over $63,000 in April 2021, increasing more than six-fold, as shown in Graph 6.1. Then the price fell more than 45 percent from its April peak, but went back up again to over $67,000 in November 2021, then

GRAPH 6.1

Source: Coinbase

fell to about $46,000 at the end of the year, and in January 2022 to $38,000, down 43 percent from its peak, but still very high. The Los Angeles Lakers re-named their basketball stadium the "Crypto.com Arena" in time for Christmas 2021.

The prices of other crypto currencies, for example Ethereum, as shown in Graph 6.2, similarly boomed, dropped, bounced and dropped.

> But why should we not let people choose freely what money they want to use? . . . I have no objection to governments issuing money, but I believe their claim to a *monopoly*, or their power to *limit* the kinds of money in which contracts may be concluded within their territory, or to determine the *rates* at which monies can be exchanged, to be wholly harmful. . . . There could be no more effective check against the abuse of money by the government than if people were free to refuse any money they distrusted and to prefer money in which they had confidence.[1]

The principal ideas and beliefs behind expanding cryptocurrencies are intended to be a challenge to, or even an assault on,

GRAPH 6.2

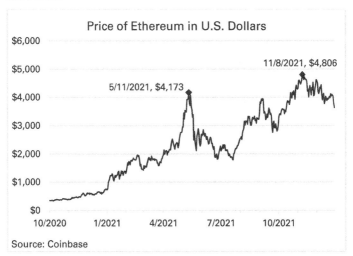

Source: Coinbase

central banks, official currencies, and established financial systems. "We are looking for alternative currencies to compete with the U.S. dollar," said one Bitcoin promoter, Zhou Xiaomeng of American CryptoFed, declaring further that "'It's the beginning of the end' for central banking and the U.S. dollar."[2]

One may wonder if it is possible for people to come to prefer cryptocurrencies like Bitcoin to central bank currencies like Federal Reserve dollars. Some people, especially those engaged in illegal activities like cyber blackmail or the use of ransomware, already do. Might others, honestly seeking Hayekian choice, use cryptocurrencies as a common means of payment, in addition to their current use as an object of what has become large-scale price speculation?

An obvious obstacle to the use of cryptocurrencies on the Bitcoin model for ordinary payments is their extreme, speculative price volatility. For example, on May 19, 2021, the day that China banned financial institutions from providing cryptocurrency services, Bitcoin experienced a 22-percent one-day decline in value. If the price of a product was expressed in dollars, then its price in Bitcoins would have gone up 28 percent that day, no doubt causing anguish to anyone contemplating using them for a major purchase. Conversely, if the seller had expressed the price in Bitcoins, it would effectively and unintentionally have cut its sales price by 22 percent that day. Such volatility seems to make Bitcoin unsuitable as a currency for normal commerce. As the Bank for International Settlements concluded, such cryptocurrencies "are speculative assets rather than money."[3]

Yet in September 2021, Bitcoin joined the U.S. dollar as legal tender in El Salvador. El Salvador is a small country, but this development was certainly interesting. Given the extreme volatility of Bitcoin prices that make it unsuitable for use in commercial transactions, El Salvador's decision seems questionable. Early reports suggested that the Bitcoin rollout in El Salvador was marred at least initially by technical glitches, consumer preference for U.S. dollars, fraud, and high user fees.[4] In November, at the Latin American Bitcoin and Blockchain Conference, it was reported that Salvadoran President Nayib Bukele "came onstage to an animation of [himself] beaming down from a flying saucer and outlined his plans for Bitcoin City: a new charter city to be built from scratch, centered on Bitcoin mining."[5] In January 2022, the International Monetary Fund, during negotiations for a proposed $1.3 billion loan to the government of El Salvador, urged it to remove Bitcoin's status as legal tender, citing financial stability and other concerns.[6] It will be instructive to see how this monetary experiment plays out.

With the explicit founding goal being to escape government currencies, central banks, and regulations, with impetus from those who believe that the existing financial infrastructure and establishment cannot be trusted, cryptocurrencies propose to replace central banks with a network of individuals with computer and marketing skills. However, central banks all over the world, including the Federal Reserve, are studying whether and how to issue digital currencies of their own. According to the Bank for International Settlements 2021 CBDC Survey, "About 60% of central banks . . . are conducting [CBDC] experiments or proofs-of-concept, while 14% are moving forward to development and pilot arrangements."[7] The EU countries have organized a task force to collaborate on the development of a digital euro; a U.K. taskforce of the Treasury and the Bank of England will examine a potential central bank digital currency; the Federal Reserve is engaged in extensive research on a U.S. digital dollar; and China leads the world in the introduction of a central bank digital currency. At the same time, China has made private cryptocurrency dealings illegal.

The ultimate results of these efforts could fundamentally turn the tables in the cryptocurrency world in favor of the central banks. It is easy to imagine a major central bank like the Fed dominating the digital currency used by the public and thereby becoming an even more concentrated, even more monopolistic monetary power than before. How all this will play out is still highly uncertain. We take up the details of these developments later in this chapter.

Designed by persons who wanted to avoid currency transfers

through established financial intermediaries such as banks and central banks, cryptocurrencies utilize a distributed ledger technology called a blockchain, which relies on people experienced in computer technology to validate financial transactions that are replicated across many locations in a computer network. A transaction is stored in multiple places to create a decentralized system that is meant to make it secure from cybercriminals seeking to hack into networks and steal assets.

In their early phase, cryptocurrencies such as Bitcoin and its numerous imitators were theoretically interesting but did not seem a threat to U.S. financial markets or financial stability. The cryptocurrency market was too small, from a macroeconomic point of view, to be a significant form of money. The 2019 FSOC Annual Report discussed cryptocurrencies but put their total market capitalization at only $209 billion in September 2019.[8] This compared to U.S. currency in circulation of $1.7 trillion and total banking assets of $18.5 trillion at the time and was not viewed as large enough to make it to the list of systemic risks to worry about. The Office of Financial Research 2019 Annual Report expressed the same view.

By 2021, however, the total cryptocurrency market capitalization soared with the bull market and at year end was $2.2 trillion, dropping during January 2022 to $1.7 trillion. It had hit a $2.4 trillion high in May 2021, gone down by half, then boomed back and fallen again.[9] The speculative energy and high volatility of cryptocurrencies are apparent and the size has become significant. The corresponding U.S. currency in circulation and total banking assets were $2.2 trillion and $22.6 trillion, respectively.

As far as actually making payments, however, as distinct from speculating on prices, many users of cryptocurrencies, by most accounts, were not and are not ordinary consumers, but often terrorists and criminals.[10] They use the technology for payments of various criminal enterprises such as terrorist activities, illegal drug networks, ransomware, and human trafficking. This could be viewed as an issue of law enforcement, not of systemic financial risk.

Cryptocurrency blockchain systems rely on the integrity of validators, or miners, to validate legitimate transactions and thus to build a blockchain that only contains actual transactions. Validators, or miners, are people with high computer skills who are rewarded, usually with deposits of cryptocurrency, for their validation efforts. However, miners may validate a blockchain regardless of whether it contains honest or criminal transactions.[11]

For a decentralized, purely electronic system, it is essential to be secure and safe from hacking, but cryptocurrencies have in fact been hacked many times. Of course, cybersecurity is a major concern not just in cryptocurrencies but throughout the financial system and in society in general.

Cryptocurrencies usefully force you to consider, Esteemed Reader, whom you should trust to control your money—your current heavily regulated and government-guaranteed bank, a possibly politicized central bank, an unaccountable group of cryptocurrency operators, or should you place your trust in gold coins in your safe? How about trusting Facebook to provide your money?

The Libra Challenge and Governments' Responses

In June 2019, Facebook, Inc., now called Meta, issued a white paper announcing that it would sponsor a new global cryptocurrency called Libra, a name subsequently changed to Diem. The Libra proposal was a major, overt, and direct challenge to existing central banks, financial institutions, and financial systems.

The Libra white paper grandiosely announced:

> Libra's mission is to enable a simple global currency and financial infrastructure that empowers billions of people.[12]

Libra would run on its own blockchain and was designed to be a "stablecoin," a digital asset designed to have a stable value that would be backed by investments in financial assets denominated in principal national currencies, in contrast to Bitcoin, which is backed by nothing. Libra would issue money-like cryptocurrency and invest in financial assets. It seemed to resemble a huge global bank, or, in a conservative form, something like a huge global multicurrency money market fund. This was more problematic. Just what kind of financial entity would it be, and what risks would it create? What kind of assets could constitute the "backing"? How high would the leverage of the entity be? We examine more closely the variable meaning of statements that stablecoins are "backed" by assets below.

The white paper stated that the world needed a reliable digital currency that would become "the internet of money." The billions of people served would include, it said, the 1.7 billion adults worldwide who do not use existing financial institutions.[13] According to the plan, Libra would be governed by an independent association based in Geneva, Switzerland, consisting of businesses, nonprofits, multilateral organizations, and academic institutions.

In other words, one of the richest and most powerful companies in the world proposed to establish a global currency with a stable price, or exchange rate, relative to a basket of national currencies, that could build on Facebook's existing network of now over 3 billion monthly users.[14] The size of the crypto market could potentially increase exponentially, operating outside the established banking systems and central banks. This got the attention of government regulators and agencies worldwide.

The issue was particularly relevant to the United States government. Going back at least to the Bretton Woods Agreement in 1944, the United States dollar has been the world's dominant reserve currency. Originally, this meant that central banks around the world would link their currencies to the dollar through fixed exchange rates, and the United States would commit to redeem dollars for gold on demand at the fixed price of one ounce of gold = \$35. This system ensured that there would always be worldwide demand to hold dollar investments.

To hold safe dollar-denominated assets, other countries principally bought United States Treasury securities. The demand for its Treasury securities allowed the United States to borrow more cheaply and led to a degree of international subsidization of the United States economy, which continues to this day. The French in the 1960s dubbed this an "exorbitant privilege," which it was and is. On the other hand, it helped finance the global military security umbrella provided by America, which others, especially Europe and Japan, relied and rely on. It thus might be viewed as a reasonable trade for them.

The situation changed radically when it became increasingly clear in the late 1960s that the dollar had become far overvalued with respect to gold and the redemption price of $35 per ounce could not be maintained. In August 1971, blaming "international currency speculators," President Nixon announced that the United States would no longer redeem dollars for gold for foreign governments: in short, the United States reneged on its Bretton Woods commitments.

This made the dollar a fiat currency, backed only by the credit of the U.S. government. Since then, in terms of gold, the dollar has depreciated by about 98 percent, as shown in Graph 6.3.

Nonetheless, the dollar has remained the world's dominant reserve currency. According to the International Monetary Fund (IMF), approximately 59 percent of all non-U.S. central bank reserves were held in U.S. dollar-denominated assets in the fourth quarter of 2020. Since the world now runs entirely on fiat currency, and the Bretton Woods system is long dead, we are all monetary Nixonians now.

The international demand for dollar securities helps keep U.S. borrowing costs and interest rates lower than they would otherwise be. As we write, U.S. government deficits have burgeoned and taken the level of U.S. debt to unprecedented and previously unimagined levels. From the viewpoint of the U.S. Treasury, the level of borrowing to finance the 2020 crisis and the continued spending in 2021 and beyond makes it more important than ever for the United States dollar to remain the world's principal reserve currency.

In his 2021 book, *Principles for Dealing with the Changing World*

GRAPH 6.3

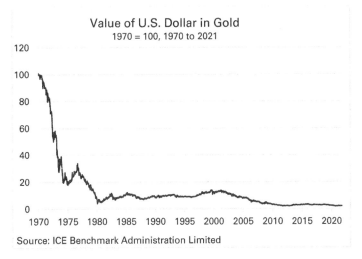

Value of U.S. Dollar in Gold
1970 = 100, 1970 to 2021

Source: ICE Benchmark Administration Limited

Order, the prominent global hedge fund manager Ray Dalio argued:

> The US's debt burdens are high, its debt is denominated in dollars, . . . so it has the ability to print money to service its debts. This reduces its risk of default but increases its devaluation risk. As you can see, if the US lost its reserve currency status, it would be in serious financial trouble.[15]

With Facebook proposing to launch a new global currency to compete with the dollar, one that could build its acceptance with the huge number of global Facebook users, could Libra or something like it potentially challenge the dollar as the world's reserve currency? What impact could that have?

As originally proposed, the Libra currency would have been governed by a group of private entities based in Switzerland, arguably outside the reach of U.S. regulation. Officials at Treasury and the Federal Reserve were concerned about that.

Other departments of the U.S. government had their own important issues. Since cryptocurrency payments are often used today by criminals, Federal law enforcement entities and the

Treasury worried that, as a Swiss-based entity, Libra would not be subject to the U.S. anticrime and anti-money laundering regime. Government agencies, including the Federal Reserve, were troubled about the privacy implications raised by giving Facebook potential access to billions of people's financial data.

Reacting to these issues, Federal Reserve Chairman Powell, in a July 2019 report to Congress, urged that Libra not be permitted to go forward until the concerns about money laundering, financial instability, and consumer privacy were addressed, stating that the Federal Reserve would have no power to apply to Libra its policy rules applicable to banks. This implies an argument that if a cryptocurrency issuer functions like a bank, it needs similar kinds of regulation as banks—an argument later formally adopted by U.S. regulators.

The regulatory questions are particularly complex: many countries are involved, and there is no unified legislative or regulatory framework in the United States for cryptocurrency. Instead, multiple agencies can regulate various aspects of the market, and jurisdictional gaps exist. For example, the Securities and Exchange Commission can only regulate cryptocurrency if it is a "security," within the meaning of Federal securities laws. Whether or not an asset like cryptocurrency is a security is legally complicated and ultimately is determined by the courts, on a case-by case-basis, after often-lengthy judicial proceedings. Even if a cryptocurrency is found to be a security, the SEC's authority is generally limited to requiring certain disclosures and to sanctioning civilly fraudulent activities.

Meanwhile, the Commodities Futures Trading Commission determined that cryptocurrency is a commodity and under some circumstances, a cryptocurrency may be deemed a derivative.[16] The CFTC's resulting authority is generally limited to antifraud and anti-manipulation enforcement. But this hardly addressed the envisioned role of Libra as a new global money. Cryptocurrencies could also run afoul of various federal and state laws governing money transfers, but most cryptocurrency activities are likely to fall outside of the patchwork of current U.S. regulatory jurisdictions.

Considering these problems, the federal agencies wanted Congress to enact legislation that would impose a comprehensive regulatory framework upon stablecoins like Libra, in particular, and upon cryptocurrencies in general. In November 2021, the President's Working Group on Financial Markets (PWG), comprising the Secretary of the Treasury and the Chairmen of the Federal Reserve, the SEC, and the CFTC, joined in this case by the Office of the Comptroller of the Currency and the Federal Deposit Insurance Corporation, issued a "Report on Stablecoins." It suggested a comprehensive system of regulation for stablecoins. The key recommendation of this PWG report is:

> Legislation should require stablecoin issuers to be insured depository institutions.[17]

That step alone would create a clear federal regulator and ensure government control over potential competitors to the dollar. It would require disclosure of complete, audited financial statements. There would be regular examination by a primary banking regulator. As we write, it is not clear how this recommendation will proceed, although Wyoming, desirous of becoming the most welcoming state for cryptocurrency issuers, has begun issuing special-purpose state banking charters for cryptocurrency operations.[18]

Previously, in July 2021, the Chairman of Congress' Joint Economic Committee had introduced legislation for comprehensive regulation of cryptocurrencies to address what he called, not without reason, the "crypto craze." The bill would "define which tokens are securities and which are commodities and gives the Treasury the power to approve dollar-backed stablecoins."[19] That would also include the power not to approve them, or presumably to disapprove those already in existence. The proposal would also authorize the Federal Reserve to issue its own central bank digital currency. The bill did not move in Congress but remains an example of directions Congress may ultimately consider.

That the concerns of U.S. government agencies about stablecoins were shared by members of Congress was apparent in 2019, when the Chair of the House Financial Services Committee wrote to Facebook management, forcefully requesting:

> That Facebook and its partners immediately agree to a moratorium on any movement forward on Libra—its proposed cryptocurrency and Calibra—its proposed digital wallet.[20] It appears that these products may lend themselves to an entirely new global financial system that is based out of Switzerland and intended to rival U.S. monetary policy and the dollar. This raises serious privacy, trading, national security, and monetary policy concerns for not only Facebook's over two billion users, but also for investors, consumers, and the broader global economy.[21]

The regulatory and political response to Libra was international. In July 2019, the G-7 finance ministers and central bank governors agreed that stablecoin projects with global footprints like Libra raise serious regulatory and systemic concerns. The Finance Ministers of Germany and France, jointly, as well as the Bank of England and the Reserve Bank of Australia, all issued their own statements of concerns.

For the next several months, Facebook management participated in numerous hearings and meetings with Congress, U.S. regulatory agencies, and international regulators, the tone of many of which could not have been very comfortable for the Facebook representatives. To an observer, it appeared that Facebook had failed to anticipate the concerns that regulators would raise and had been either too naïve or remarkably aggressive about the government reactions the Libra proposal would engender.

Faced with a storm of international governmental pressure, Facebook made major alterations to its proposal, including changing the name from Libra to Diem, and issued a revised white paper in April 2020—in the midst of the Covid financial crisis.

The theme of this new approach was conciliatory. The renamed Diem would be designed to "marry blockchain technology with accepted regulatory frameworks" and "to integrate smoothly with local monetary and macroprudential policies." A principal change was that instead of offering a single, global multicurrency unit of account or "coin," Diem would also issue single-currency coins, such as Libra U.S. Dollar and Libra Euro. Each single-currency coin would be backed by a reserve of short-term assets such as bank deposits in the currency in which the coin is denominated or short-term government securities denominated in that currency. There would still be a global, multicurrency coin, but that would be a "digital composite" of the single-currency coins, with each single currency being given some weighting. Exactly how this was supposed to work is not clear to us.

Facebook then said that it

> would welcome the oversight and control . . . by a group of regulators and central banks or an international organization (e.g., IMF) under the guidance of the Association's main supervisory authority, the Swiss Financial Market Supervisory Authority (FINMA).

A key theme of the revised white paper was Diem's commitment to a regulatory compliance framework that would "meet or exceed" all relevant laws and requirements, presumably meeting the regulatory requirements of every nation in the world, since Diem was intended to be a global network. Additionally, the white paper expressed the hope that central banks would develop their own central bank digital currencies and that these CBDCs could be directly integrated into the Libra network.

In her 2021 book, *Cryptocurrencies: Money, Trust and Regulation*, Oonagh McDonald, a former member of the U.K. parliament, U.K. bank regulator, and author, was sharply critical of cryptocurrency as a payments technology and of the Libra/Diem proposals.[22] Among her criticisms was that the new single-currency Diem stablecoin was simply a proxy for existing currencies. Why, she asked, would anyone presumably pay a fee to convert a dollar or a Euro into the stablecoin version and then another fee to eventually convert it back into the same currency? She doubted that any central bank that had developed its own CBDC would cooperate and share monetary power with a non-bank, profit-making enterprise. She questioned the role for Libra-Diem in terms of the underbanked. She was skeptical about whether Libra-Diem would actually be a faster, cheaper, or more efficient system for international payments than the systems already in place or being developed and suggested that it would be more productive to direct efforts to the improvement of speed in current payment systems rather than toward "the risky superstructure" proposed by Facebook. She expressed grave concern about the privacy implications arising from Facebook gaining access to the vast amount of personal financial information that would be part of the new network.

McDonald further pointed out that the different types of costs associated with stablecoins often are unclear and high. Ethereum users have to purchase Ethereum's token, Ether, in order to use the blockchain. Cryptocurrency issuers and exchanges impose fees for buying cryptocurrency and for moving money into a cryptocurrency or a fiat currency. Other operating charges apply as well, and international stablecoin transactions are quite expensive. No interest is paid on most stablecoins, so in most cases, the stablecoin issuer keeps all the interest it earns on reserves for itself (although as we write some are beginning to pay interest). Requiring cryptocurrency issuers and exchanges to let users understand the fees they will be charged would be a benefit of appropriate regulation of cryptocurrency.

On top of the open challenge to central banks, the regulatory impediments to the implementation of the Libra-Diem ideas were formidable, to say the least. When Facebook submitted an application to FINMA "for a payment system license . . . on the basis of the updated whitepaper," FINMA replied in April 2020:

> The outcome and duration of the procedure remain open . . .
> FINMA will now thoroughly analyse the application . . . it
> will impose extra requirements for additional services that
> pose increased risks. This applies in particular to bank-like
> risks. In addition, FINMA will give special consideration to
> whether strict national and international standards for pay-

ment infrastructures and also for combating money laundering can be upheld. . . .

FINMA has always emphasised that the planned international scope of the project requires an internationally coordinated approach. Accordingly, FINMA has been in close contact with the Swiss National Bank and more than 20 other supervisory authorities and central banks from around the world since the start of its dealings with the Libra project.[23]

That was a bureaucratic formula for no action anytime soon.

Facebook then stated that it would only proceed after all relevant regulatory approvals were obtained. Presumably, this included regulatory approvals in a very large number of countries, since its operations were to be worldwide. Anyone familiar with intergovernmental processes, let alone multinational governmental processes, would not underestimate the time this would take and how difficult it would be to obtain the requisite approvals in a world of complicated and often inconsistent national regulatory regimes.

Apparently recognizing the impracticality of achieving its goals due to the enormous regulatory hurdles, in May 2021 Libra-Diem announced a major scaling back of its proposal. It then planned to relocate its operations to the United States, abandon its FINMA application, and limit itself, at least initially, to issuing only a U.S. dollar denominated stablecoin and registering as a money services business with the U.S. Treasury's Financial Crimes Enforcement Network. The Diem U.S. dollar stablecoin would be issued exclusively through Silver Gate Bank, a U.S. regulated bank. So, instead of a revolutionary global private currency, Diem had become just another bank payments product.

Finally, in January 2022, Facebook threw in the towel completely, announcing that Diem would wind down and sell its technology to Silver Gate. The saga of Libra-Diem indicates the virtual impossibility of even one of the largest, most sophisticated tech companies in the world setting up a private currency that would challenge existing national currencies when faced with governmental hostility and regulatory impediments.

**Evolving Approaches to the Regulation
of Private Stablecoins**

Meanwhile, a variety of private stablecoins, such as Tether and USDC, have proliferated. Governments have almost universally reacted to the advent of private stablecoins by demonstrating a strong desire to regulate them. We examine the reasons for this government interest and contrast the evolving approaches to the regulation of stablecoins taken by the United States and China.

Why are governments anxious to regulate stablecoins? The November 2021 President's Working Group Report, seeks extensive regulation for three stated reasons: to address risks to stablecoin users and to guard against stablecoin runs; to address concerns about payment system risks; and to address additional concerns about systemic risk and concentration of economic power.[24] There is a fourth essential but unmentioned reason: to control potential competitors to the official currency.

One purpose of any government regulation is to protect its citizens from fraud, and the first argument for regulation advanced by the PWG fits squarely within this rubric. To fully understand it, we must return to the sometimes elusive concept of what it may mean for a stablecoin to be "backed by" dollar-denominated assets. To a layman, the term "backed by" implies that the holder of a stablecoin has the ability to redeem the coin for dollars. That is not always the case with stablecoins. The President's Working Group Report notes that while some stablecoin issuers impose no limits on the ability of a holder to redeem, others set minimum redemption amounts that in some instances may be more than the amount held by typical users. Further, even if the value of a particular stablecoin is equaled by its reserve, other creditors may compete with the stablecoin holders for the reserve assets.[25]

Tether and USDC, two of the largest stablecoin issuers, claim to be fully backed by U.S. dollar assets in their reserves. Professor Lawrence White of George Mason University points out that while both companies speak of redeeming their coins at a dollar each, the contracts governing these stablecoins contain escape clauses significantly limiting this right.[26] For instance, Tether allows itself to delay redemptions due to losses, illiquidity, or unavailability of its reserves and to redeem Tether coins by distributing reserves rather than converting the reserves into dollars. Tether also charges for redemption and has a large minimum redemption value of $100,000. So perhaps, just when you really want your dollars back, you won't be able to get them. This is analogous to banks under the gold standard, which promised redemption of your deposits in gold, but if things got tough, you discovered that the banks "stopped payment" (as it was called) instead.

Professor White concludes that these provisions make stablecoins vulnerable to bank-style runs. If people fear there won't be enough to go around, they will line up at the virtual doors to get their dollars out first.

There is often no clarity about what types of dollar-denominated assets are contained in stablecoin reserves. Are they deposits in high quality banks and short-term Treasury securities, or are they junk bonds and low-rated commercial paper, or maybe loans to affiliated entities or other cryptocurrencies? Many stablecoin issuers are opaque about the makeup of their reserves. An obvious reform would be a standard imposing the publication of full, audited financial statements. These would include the specific assets held in stablecoin reserves. Furnishing stablecoin holders with audited financial statements would also provide more clarity about redemption. Protecting stablecoin holders from concealed risk is a valid reason for requiring clear information, just as with the disclosures required by securities regulation.

The second reason for regulation espoused by the President's Working Group is to address concerns about payment system risks. The PWG report suggests that stablecoins operating as payment systems need to be protected from the operational, settlement, and liquidity risks common to all payment systems.

These risks are perhaps exacerbated because some stablecoins do not rely on their operators to manage payments, but use "defi," a system in which the users of a payment system interact directly, without any third-party balance sheet as operator or mediator.

The third reason—to address concerns about systemic risk and concentrations of commercial power—reflects the same government concerns that were raised by the Libra-Diem proposal. If large numbers of people use stablecoins, and stablecoin issuers are subject to runs, they could have a disruptive impact on the financial system in times of stress.

The PWG report is disingenuous by not explicitly addressing the potential threat to the dollar, which was certainly a Treasury and Federal Reserve concern with Libra-Diem and is with stablecoins in general.

At least some stablecoin reforms appear highly desirable, especially making sure that stablecoin holders have audited financial statements, clearly communicated redemption conditions, and transparency about the nature and risks of their investment.

China's Approach versus the U.S. Approach to Regulation

In dealing with the issues raised by stablecoins, China and the United States, at least as reflected by the recommendations in the President's Working Group Report, are going in different directions. The Chinese approach is to prohibit all private cryptocurrency transactions for its citizens, except for participation in the government's own digital yuan. On September 24, 2021, in a statement posted on its website, China's central bank declared all cryptocurrency transactions to be illegal. Specifically naming Bitcoin, Ether, and Tether, the central bank decreed that cryptocurrency should not be circulated and used in the market as currency. It also said it was illegal for overseas exchanges to provide services for Chinese residents through the internet, having already prohibited cryptocurrency exchanges from operating in China several years ago. The statement spoke of implementing a comprehensive monitoring system involving all levels of government and of the need to investigate employees of foreign cryptocurrency exchanges advertising their services in China.[27] The Chinese apparently intended to eliminate cryptocurrency as a means by which savings could leave China and to eliminate all competition with official Chinese currency, both paper and digital. This statist and authoritarian approach is certainly one way to avoid the problems with stablecoins laid out in the President's Working Group report and to reinforce the government's currency monopoly—an approach not discussed in the PWG paper.

The PWG recommended a less draconian, three-part approach for the U.S. As noted above, it proposed that all stablecoin issuers be required to be government-insured depository institutions. That would make them subject to "appropriate supervision and regulation" at both the depository institution and the holding company levels. This is a not unreasonable idea because, when issuing stablecoins, issuers are functioning as a bank: they are providing currency just as a bank does when it takes deposits, and they are investing the funds received as assets to support their liabilities, just as a bank does. Declines in the value of the assets and then the customers being unable to get their money back is the most classic banking risk.

With such a regulatory structure, stablecoin issuers would have to confront the fact that the power to regulate involves the power to destroy, to paraphrase Chief Justice Marshall's famous statement about taxation. Regulators, presumably the three federal banking agencies, the Federal Reserve, the Comptroller of the Currency, and the Federal Deposit Insurance Corporation, would be empowered to charter stablecoin issuers as banks. Devising "appropriate" regulations would be controversial and political but certainly doable. However, bank regulators may be too stringent and unintentionally, or intentionally, destroy this growing business.

Many regulatory questions would have to be addressed. A major one is the question of what capital requirements would be imposed on stablecoin banks. Presumably, these banks would be required to pay for deposit insurance, like other banks. They would have to hire many people to ensure regulatory compliance. How would these new costs affect their profitability and their ultimate viability? Would there be limits on their expansion and the types of entities they can own or be owned by? The U.S. financial system imposes many varieties of regulation, and regulation as an insured depository institution is the most stringent. Would the stablecoin industry be able to thrive, or survive, in that environment?

Concerning payment system risk, the PWG would require custodial digital wallet providers to be subject to "appropriate" federal oversight. It would give the federal banking supervisor of the stablecoin issuer the authority to require that any entity the issuer deals with must also meet appropriate risk management standards, if the entity is critical to the functioning of the stablecoin arrangement. Concerning systemic risk issues, the PWG proposes to restrict stablecoin issuers', and maybe digital wallet providers', affiliations with commercial entities, just as banks and bank holding companies are restricted.

In sum, the PWG calls for an extensive system of regulation by powerful regulators for entities involved in stablecoins, which those entities would doubtless regard as onerous, perhaps oppressive. Despite calls from the industry to provide a single regulator for everything related to stablecoins, the PWG plan envisions a continuation of the United States' fragmented approach to financial regulation; stablecoin issuers would have a bank regulator and also be subject to regulation by other federal agencies, like the SEC, the CFTC, and the Consumer Financial Protection Bureau.

To create the regulatory system envisioned by the PWG would require legislation. Getting legislation through Congress would have an uncertain, perhaps lengthy timeline. As a backup, the PWG suggests that if Congress does not act, the Financial Stability Oversight Council should designate stablecoin activities as systemically important risks. The six participants in the PWG report are all voting members of FSOC, so presumably this could be arranged. If this happened, the Federal Reserve would gain broad regulatory authority over stablecoin activities in one fell swoop. One might characterize this as the issuer of the official U.S. currency getting regulatory control over its potential competitors.

Early in this chapter, we quoted Hayek, who argued that people ought to be free to choose between state and private currencies. Indeed, one perspective from which to consider cryptocurrency is the broad question of whether or not a currency should be the exclusive province of the government. China (not a Hayekian nation!) has chosen to absolutely foreclose all private currency and to keep money a purely state attribute. The United States seems to be following a regulatory approach, but the burden of regulation might ultimately overwhelm the stablecoin industry and produce the same result as in China.

Blockchain technology and decentralized finance certainly have the capacity for innovations in the payment process. But do the risks and downsides of stablecoins outweigh their benefits, which appear to largely be technological improvements, perhaps yet to be achieved, to improve the speed and cost of payments? Can these benefits be realized by ongoing improvement in existing payments systems, as Oonagh McDonald suggests, without needing a cryptocurrency? Not all new technologies survive. (The Betamax languishing in Howard's basement closet demonstrates this last proposition.)

In the meantime, central banks keep working on how they can issue their own digital currency.

Central Bank Digital Currency

A deeply ironic twist in the cryptocurrency saga is the increasing discussion and development of central bank digital currency (CBDC). Bitcoin was introduced as an alternative to central bank currencies in 2009 with a good deal of the motivation behind its creation being distrust of central banks. But then many central banks began studying the possibility of issuing their own cryptocurrency. These studies are now far advanced. Since the potential result would be an official government currency, it would by definition not be a "crypto" currency, but a "central bank digital currency."

As early as 2014, the Chinese government, apparently fearing that the circulation of global cryptocurrencies inside China could undermine Chinese control of its citizens and its own monetary system, began to study a Chinese official digital currency.[28] This digital currency, the digital yuan, was rolled out beginning in April 2021 in a dozen Chinese cities as a trial.[29] In these cities, the digital yuan is available on mobile phones or on cards, with a silhouette of Mao showing on the screen or card, and can be used by Chinese consumers to make payments. Transactions in digital yuan are controlled entirely by the Chinese central bank. The head of the project at the Chinese central bank explained that this is "in order to protect our currency sovereignty and legal currency status."[30]

China's development of its CBDC has apparently motivated the Federal Reserve and other central banks to step up their own level of research and experimentation.

China seems to have two goals in pioneering the digital yuan for use domestically and internationally. Domestically, the digital yuan is a means for an authoritarian government to further control the Chinese population. The digital yuan uses only the central bank and a few approved banks in China as financial intermediaries, and the central bank's power is assured. This system presumably will enable the Chinese Communist Party to see every financial transaction paid for in digital yuan. The central bank's control over digital yuan accounts would allow the government to confiscate the funds of, or cut off access to the payments system by, any digital yuan holder who engages in any activity the Chinese Communist Party views as subversive.

The second goal of the Chinese in developing the digital yuan is international: to directly challenge the dominance of the U.S. dollar. As of April 2019, the dollar was the currency used in 88 percent of international foreign exchange transactions, while the yuan was used in only four percent of such transactions, according to the Bank for International Settlements.[31] China hopes that the digital yuan can become an alternative to the dollar for use in international transactions.

You might ask, Perceptive Reader, why anyone not in China would choose to give the Chinese Communist Party control over their money. An excellent question!

One answer can be found in the U.S. policy of sanctioning those the U.S. government believes to be terrorists or engaged in criminal activities. The U.S. Treasury's data base of sanctioned individuals and firms, the "Specially Designated Nationals and Blocked Persons List," comprises persons and entities located virtually anywhere in the world, including more than 250 Chinese persons and entities.[32] As the issuer of dollars that the world's banks need to transact business, the United States government has long demanded and received access from banks to information about international transactions, which it has used to impose sanctions on a large number of people and organizations. Even banks in Switzerland, once the staunchest defender of bank secrecy, now open their books to the U.S. government. SWIFT, the messaging network that commercial banks use to transfer money among themselves internationally, can also be monitored by the U.S. government. The combination of these factors has enabled the United States to punish those whom it deems to be bad actors by preventing banks from doing business with them and freezing their assets. Opponents of this U.S. policy have not unreasonably described it as "dollar weaponization."

Who would use the digital yuan? Countries, individuals, and entities who have more reason to distrust the United States than China. These could include entities of the governments of countries unfriendly to the United States, such as Iran, Venezuela, North Korea, or Cuba, and perhaps those governments that have borrowed extensively under the Chinese Belt and Road Program, whose finances are thus to some extent tied to the Chinese government. According to the Council on Foreign Relations, as of March 2021, 139 countries, or about 70 percent of all the countries in the world, were formally affiliated with Belt and Road,

including 39 countries in sub-Saharan Africa, 34 in Europe and
Central Asia, 25 in East Asia and the Pacific, 18 in Latin America
and the Caribbean, 17 in the Middle East and North Africa, and
six in South Asia.[33] China's financial influence may be particularly strong with countries in the initiative that the Council cate-
gorizes as low income.[34] These nations, entities, and persons may
want to use the digital yuan to evade U.S.-imposed sanctions or
to transact business with their creditor, China, thereby weaken-
ing the global reach of the United States and making it more difficult to implement American policy.

Faced with the launch of the digital yuan, the Federal Reserve
had no choice but to accelerate exploration of its own digital currency. Chairman Powell in February 2021 Senate testimony
described researching a digital dollar as "a very high priority."[35]
The Federal Reserve would of course need to create an entirely
secure digital currency—a major challenge, given successful
cyberattacks over the last several years on what were thought
to be very secure government systems, in particularly the Solar
Winds hack of 2020.

In January 2022, the Federal Reserve issued a discussion paper
entitled, "Money and Payments: The U.S. Dollar in the Age of
Digital Transformation," intended to be "the first step in a public
discussion between the Federal Reserve and stakeholders about
central bank digital currencies."[36] This thoughtful and very carefully worded paper is neutral about whether or not the Federal
Reserve favors issuing a digital currency and emphasizes that the
Federal Reserve would not implement a digital dollar without
congressional authorization.

The paper identifies benefits and risks of a central bank digital
dollar. Among the potential benefits: A digital dollar could meet
needs for payment services with a currency that is free from credit
and liquidity risk and provide public access to safe, central bank
money in digital as well as paper form. It might streamline cross-
border payments and enhance economic inclusion. Revealing
what we believe is most important to the Federal Reserve and the
U.S. government, the discussion paper, unlike the PWG Report

on stablecoins, expressly acknowledges that a digital dollar could support the international primacy of the U.S. dollar.[37]

On the risks and downsides, the paper suggests a principal risk is that a digital dollar could reduce deposits in financial institutions and the supply of short-term funding instruments. This could increase bank funding expenses, reduce credit availability, raise credit costs to businesses and households, and disrupt the short-term funding markets, including money market mutual funds and the market for U.S. Treasury securities. By providing an easily available super-safe financial refuge in troubled times, a digital dollar could also increase the likelihood and severity of runs on financial institutions, since bank deposit holders and money market fund investors might immediately move their money out of banks and money market funds into the safety of accounts with the Federal Reserve. Finally, the discussion paper recognizes that, since a digital dollar would reveal users' financial transactions transparently to the government, it would be tricky to balance protecting privacy with the need to maintain cybersecurity and prevent money laundering and other criminal activities.[38]

The Federal Reserve's paper has no explicit proposals or recommendation; it asks for public comments on the issues involved. Alex submitted a comment pointing out that the paper does not address at all the essential question of what assets the central bank would acquire with its new CBDC deposits.

Always in the background is the big question: Will the digital yuan or other official digital currencies erode the role of the dollar as the world's dominant reserve currency? The widespread interest in CBDCs by other central banks, as well as by global public entities such as the IMF and private entities like SWIFT, is one impetus for the United States to create its own digital currency. Among the many other countries in some stage of exploring a digital currency are Switzerland, Australia, Turkey, the Bahamas (already launched), Brazil, and Estonia, according to CBDC Tracker.[39]

The 2020 Annual Meetings of the International Monetary Fund and the World Bank Group featured a panel discussion about CBDCs. IMF Managing Director Kristalina Georgieva enthusiastically extolled the virtues of CBDCs, because of their alleged potential to bring financial services to the approximately 1.7 billion people in the world without bank accounts and because of the perceived technological potential for speeding up and making cheaper international payments. It does appear that in countries that do not have a viable system of private institutions, a CBDC might help to bring desirable financial services to the public, and further, that a Federal Reserve-run, dollar-based CBDC might be more secure and reliable than one run by many other countries' central banks.

The same factors that cause U.S. dollar paper currency to be used in numerous countries also apply to CBDCs. But in most countries, we expect governments to resist foreign CBDCs and promote their own CBDCs, as part of the sovereign power to issue money. Countries that have viable financial systems and currencies will not want to have another country's currency in wide domestic use in digital or any other form, for the same reasons they want their own central bank in the first place.

The movement toward CBDCs appears real and cannot be ignored. We believe that a U.S. CBDC is unfortunately likely, the Federal Reserve's carefully noncommittal paper notwithstanding, for two reasons. First, to repeat, the Federal Reserve and the Treasury must be concerned with preserving the primacy of the U.S. dollar as the world's reserve currency, in view of potential competition from foreign CBDCs, their widespread development, and particularly in view of the rollout of the digital yuan. Second, we observe that bureaucracies usually find ways to enhance their own power when they can.

We say this is unfortunate because it would greatly increase the already enormous power of the Federal Reserve. The Federal Reserve's resultant potential ability to directly monitor and control what should be private financial transactions, and to powerfully direct the allocation of credit, should be extremely troubling for any believer in a free society.

Cryptocurrencies vs. CBDCs

Among the issues raised by private cryptocurrencies like Tether or the formerly proposed Diem, but not by the digital dollar, is the argument that supporting cryptocurrencies is at odds with the interests of the United States. If, as a financial patriot, you wish to maintain the financial strength of the United States, you will support continuing the dollar's role as the principal reserve currency, along with the "exorbitant privilege" that entails.

Could cryptocurrencies actually succeed in replacing national currencies? The end of the Libra-Diem effort casts doubt on the ability of any private cryptocurrency, even one backed by large and influential private companies, to supplant established national currencies in the face of determined opposition from powerful governmental entities.

We have discussed the volatility problem of the Bitcoin model, a problem stablecoins avoid by being designed by definition to have a stable price in dollars or other national currency. However, being by definition tied to that fiat currency, the stablecoin automatically shares the loss of purchasing power from inflation in the reference currency. The stablecoin has thus not escaped the Federal Reserve or other central bank at all. It does seem that a stablecoin can be more accurately described as a payment product rather than as a new currency.

In addition, we have discussed how the value of the "reserve" assets of the stablecoin issuers might depreciate through credit, interest rate, or liquidity risks, perhaps by a lot, just as happens with banks, so there is the inevitable possibility of a significant difference in the par price of the stablecoin and the value of the assets backing it, a problem stressed by all financial regulators examining the question.

In the end, governments can severely restrict, regulate, tax, or punish cryptocurrency use whenever they decide to. This has already happened in China. We have described the President's Working Group's proposals for imposing extensive regulation in the U.S. In historical context, we may recall that the U.S. government taxed state bank notes out of existence in the 1860s. For 2020 and 2021 income taxes, the U.S. personal income tax form 1040 prominently requires each taxpayer to answer this question: "At any time during the year, did you receive, sell, send, exchange or otherwise acquire any financial interest in any virtual currency?" You must check Yes or No. Giving a false answer here is a criminal offense. (We anticipate that any future use of the U.S. government's own digital currency would be excepted from such reporting—the government would already know that you were using it.)

This leads us to conclude that, overall, the long-term success of CBDCs issued by major central banks in competition with cryptocurrencies appears much more likely than the replacement of government fiat currencies by cryptocurrencies, including private stablecoins. When an established government, with no need to make a profit, determines to establish a financial product and puts its political power behind making that product successful, it becomes almost impossible for a private entity to compete. This is in spite of the fact that where there is a well-established system of private financial intermediaries, there are strong fundamental reasons not to have CBDCs.

CBDCs would further centralize power in central banks, including the Federal Reserve in particular, and make it hard for private citizens to maintain any privacy from government snooping in their financial lives. If deposits are dominated or monopolized by the central bank, it must have assets to match the new deposits. This could mean a central bank role in deciding which businesses and individuals receive loans. In other words, CBDCs could centralize credit allocation in the central bank, politicizing credit decisions and turning the central bank into a government lending bank. It might, for example, prioritize loans to industries liked by the politicians currently in office and cut off credit to those they don't like. All governments like to direct and control credit for political purposes, but the global record of government banks with politicized lending is dismal. It doubtless would be again.

CBDCs could thereby reverse more than a century of positive central bank evolution which has usefully divided the issuer of base money from private credit decisions. In the process, they would subject private banks to vastly unequal and losing competition with the government's central bank.

Nonetheless, as stated above, the development of competing CBDCs from other countries, notably the digital yuan, will likely be a reason for the Federal Reserve to roll out its own CBDC, as a form of the U.S. dollar, to defend its role as the dominant world currency and principal global reserve asset.

In short, one of the surprises of the 2020s is that a libertarian revolt against central banks in the form of cryptocurrencies looks to be taken over by central banks instead and may well end up vastly increasing and centralizing central bank and government power.

CHAPTER 7

Banks

Not Their Turn This Time

THE BANKING SYSTEM got a good scare in the Covid panic, as the banks contemplated extremely large potential loan losses. During 2020, banks dramatically increased their provisions for credit losses[1] by $393 billion to total provisions for the year of $428 billion, up 214 percent from the $136 billion in 2019. This is shown in Graph 7.1. There was plenty of risk, but, of course, nobody knew what would actually happen, since there was also vast uncertainty.

GRAPH 7.1

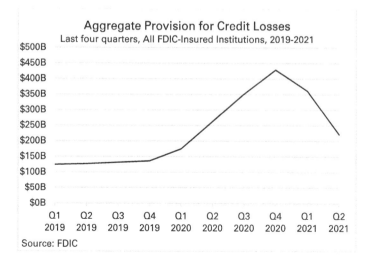

Aggregate Provision for Credit Losses
Last four quarters, All FDIC-Insured Institutions, 2019-2021

Source: FDIC

Bank profits fell sharply, reflecting the higher loan loss provisions and the low interest rate environment, which compressed bank net interest margins. With the intense uncertainty and fear of what might happen, bank stock prices dropped like a rock. They fell almost by half in a month during the Covid panic, as shown in Graph 2.4 in Chapter 2, which we repeat here as Graph 7.2.

After their bottom in March 2020, bank stock prices went sideways at about 35 percent under their pre-panic level for seven months, even while stocks in general had taken off in their post-panic boom. But in late 2020, the fear abated, and in November, bank stock prices began a powerful recovery that took them back up by 82 percent, as shown in Graph 7.3, to over their pre-panic level.

Thus, by mid-2021, banks had emerged from the Covid crisis with their stock prices fully recovered. They were busy reversing the provisions for credit losses they had made in 2020, liquidating loss reserves and taking them back into reported profits. The level of once-expected loan losses had not happened. Indeed, at 0.27 percent of total loans and leases, net charge-offs in the second quarter of 2021 were the lowest since the FDIC's Quarterly Banking Profile began in 1984.[2]

GRAPH 7.2

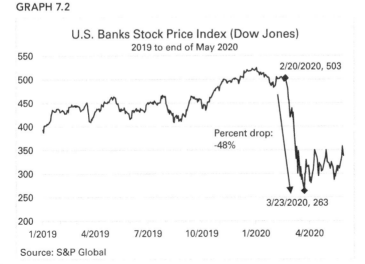

U.S. Banks Stock Price Index (Dow Jones)
2019 to end of May 2020

Source: S&P Global

GRAPH 7.3

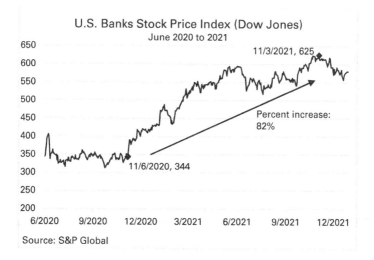

U.S. Banks Stock Price Index (Dow Jones)
June 2020 to 2021

11/3/2021, 625

Percent increase: 82%

11/6/2020, 344

Source: S&P Global

By January 2022, the *Wall Street Journal* could write, "the doomsday scenarios that banks girded against in the pandemic's early days never materialized."[3] But in the midst of the crisis, those scenarios seemed all too probable. In this context, we must wonder what the banks' loan losses would have been without the massive government interventions and bailouts of the economy in general. Certainly the losses would have been much larger, but just how much larger is a matter for counterfactual speculation.

Thus, banks appear to have emerged from the Covid crisis pretty unscathed, relative to the fears. But the great asset price inflation, built on the abnormally low interest rates created by the Federal Reserve and other central banks to survive the crisis, has generated significant risks going forward. The low rates have induced investors to reach for yield, resulting in booming leveraged corporate debt. The runaway house price inflation raises questions about housing finance. Meanwhile, the ongoing costs of the crisis, including uncertain patterns of future use of office space, continue to work their way through commercial real estate credit.

Before the pandemic, in 2019, overall delinquency rates at the largest U.S. banks had reached their lowest levels since 2001. Despite the pandemic, bank delinquencies remained low through 2020, largely because of emergency programs of loan forbearance, which meant that non-paying borrowers were not reported as delinquent; stimulus grants to households and businesses; and deferral of tax payments otherwise due.

During the crisis, deposit levels soared at banks as part of the flight to cash and safety, as people sought the government guarantee provided by federal deposit insurance. Businesses, fearing a tightening of credit, drew down their revolving credit lines, often depositing the proceeds in banks. The eight large U.S. banks deemed to be U.S. "global systemically important banks" (G-SIBs) particularly benefited from this deposit influx, since they are perceived as being "too big to fail." Financial actors felt confident having deposits at those banks that exceeded the dollar limits for federal deposit insurance. As a result, the G-SIBs were able to pay lower interest rates on those deposits than other banks.

Is that perception of safety accurate? Are the G-SIBs indeed too big to fail? The answer is Yes. This is despite all of the claims from politicians after the passage of the Dodd-Frank Act in 2010 that no bank was now too big to fail. The simple fact is that no Secretary of the Treasury, Federal Reserve Chairman, responsible bank regulator, U.S. President, or their peers in any other country would allow banks like JPMorgan, Bank of America, Citigroup, Wells Fargo, Goldman Sachs, or similar G-SIBs in other countries to fail, whatever they might say when times are calm. In times of severe financial stress, would any holder of such a high national office take the risk of triggering a resultant systemic disaster? Would any take the personal risk of the historical ignominy of being the one who presided over a resulting financial collapse? The answer is No.

The G-SIBs' size and interconnectedness with other institutions dwarf the former Lehman Brothers' systemic significance, but allowing Lehman to fail in 2008 set off a panic and came very close to sinking the economy. That panic triggered other bailouts, some of the largest in history, including the $700 billion "TARP" program, in which the Treasury made equity investments in banks and others.[4] This means that all the deposits of the G-SIBs, not just those explicitly covered by federal deposit insurance, have an implicit but real government guarantee. It is just like the one Fannie Mae and Freddie Mac also benefit from, the reality of which was demonstrated when the Treasury bailed them out, too.

A result of this implicit but real guarantee is that the size of G-SIB balance sheets has expanded, to the detriment of regional and community banks, as depositors with balances in excess of the FDIC limits very rationally flee to the G-SIBs with their deposits in times of stress. This also has the result of bolstering G-SIB profitability, since the G-SIBs can pay lower interest rates on their deposits than regional and community banks can, because G-SIB deposits are perceived to be, and actually are, safer.

Even though the Covid crisis pressured bank profitability and sank banks' stock prices, only a handful of U.S. banks failed during the Covid pandemic. This was in sharp contrast to the aftermath of the Housing Bubble, when 448 banks failed. It contrasts even more strongly to the multiple financial crises in the years 1982–92, when over 2,800 federally insured financial institutions failed—255 failures per year, or about five per week, over an extended period of eleven years. This is shown in Table 7.4.

Why was this? First, the two previous periods of financial stress lasted much longer: years, instead of less than one year. Second, there were record government subsidies financed with elas-

TABLE 7.4

Failures of FDIC-Insured Institutions in Crisis Times

	1982–1992	2009–2012	2020–2021Q2
Number of FDIC-insured institutions (average)	16,580	7,528	4,977
Total failures, including assistance transactions (sum)	2,808	448	4
Average failures per year	255	112	3
Failures as a % of institutions	16.9%	6.0%	0.1%

Source: FDIC Bank Data and Statistics.

tic currency this time, bigger than any previously. Third, after the 2007–08 crisis, banks became relatively risk averse, facing higher levels of regulatory capital and liquidity requirements, and regulatory scrutiny of risk through stress testing. This relative conservatism, combined with a long economic expansion, was reflected in the low delinquency rates and a significant increase in overall bank capital levels.

The political, regulatory, and management reactions to the 2007–09 financial crisis drove a great deal of risk out of the banking system, although commercial real estate loans, which are always risky and became a riskier asset class as a result of the Covid pandemic and lockdowns, are an exception to this trend. At the same time, overall levels of non-financial corporate debt were rising to their highest levels ever, with increasing amounts of it highly leveraged. If this risk was being pushed out of the banking system, where did it go?

Recall, Thoughtful Reader, that a key way to manage your own risk is to give it to someone else. Sophisticated, more prudent financial actors find ways to package the risks and sell them to others, perhaps less prudent and more aggressive, or perhaps less competent. The role of a salesman of risky securities may be cynically described as finding the biggest suckers.

In this respect, the corporate lending markets fundamentally changed over the past three decades. Previously, corporate loans were almost exclusively originated by banks and held on their balance sheets or syndicated to other banks. Corporate loans were not held by the general public, although there were always publicly traded corporate bonds. Increasingly, however, non-bank investors hold corporate loans through mutual funds or collateralized loan obligations (CLOs), which are vehicles that pool riskier corporate loans and issue against them securities that have different priorities with respect to the cash flows of the pool. These various credit tranches carry credit ratings ranging from the highest to the lowest. A growing number of these corporate loans are so-called leveraged loans, which FSOC has defined as "a type of loan that is extended to companies that already have considerable amounts of debt and/or have a non-investment grade credit rating or are unrated and/or whose post-financing leverage significantly exceeds industry norms or historical levels."[5]

The movement of riskier corporate debt out of the banking system and into securities markets creates a new type of financial stability risk. The failure of non-bank lenders and CLOs might be deemed preferable to bank failures because, unlike banks, they fall outside the government's guarantee and taxpayer exposure. But contemplating the possible impact of widespread failures in this market puts us in terra incognita. With $1.6 trillion in leveraged loans outstanding as of June 2021, the systemic effects of a crisis failure of a significant number of participants in this sector are simply unknown. We can only speculate about whether the links these credits have to the rest of the financial system would result in wider systemic stress. We do know that, by design, they create very high leverage—a feature vulnerable to economic shocks, by definition.

We also know that, while a large portion of the risks created by leveraged loans have been sold by banks, banks still retain a good deal of leveraged loan risk. Leveraged loans are usually divided into a revolving loan component, which banks typically retain, and a term loan component, which banks more and more sell to CLOs and other investors. In 2019, FSOC estimated that, with respect to the approximately $1.1 trillion of leveraged loans outstanding that had been originated by banks and sold to investors as of the fourth quarter of 2018, banks retained $500 billion to $600 billion of revolving loan exposure.[6] Banks also retain interests in the CLO loans they originate, although in the more highly rated tranches, and they have additional exposure to the leveraged loan market because they also typically lend to nonbank leveraged loan originators and CLOs themselves. This leveraged loan exposure is largely in the large banks, since they make most of the loans to this sector. So, one must conclude that a credit shock, say a deep recession, with widespread defaults in the leveraged loan market could have a serious negative impact on the largest commercial banks, in spite of their shifting much of the credit risk to other investors. This did not happen in the 2020 crisis, but there is always the question of next time.

During the Covid crisis, many corporate borrowers, anticipating possible liquidity problems, drew down their revolving lines of credit in advance, thereby increasing the banking system's exposure to corporate debt. In addition, $792 billion of federal Paycheck Protection Program (PPP) loans were made during the pandemic. These factors resulted in bank corporate loan growth of over 20 percent from April through July of 2020 compared to 2019, although many of these revolving loans were paid down later in 2020 and the PPP loans were largely forgiven, thereby turning the loans into a government budget expense with corresponding Treasury debt.

In the Covid panic, new issuances of leveraged loans virtually stopped. Leveraged loan default rates increased to 8.5 percent in the third quarter of 2020 from 3.4 percent in 2019, and business bankruptcies increased. Despite these increases, the historically low interest rates and CLO structures with generally larger subordinated tranches, which better enable the losses to be absorbed before investment grade tranches are impacted, combined to mitigate problems in this sector.

During the economic recovery, buoyed by continuing low interest rates and the growing demand for yields fostered by the Everything Bubble, the corporate debt market rebounded with a vengeance. Nonfinancial corporate debt reached $11.2 trillion at the end of June 2021, equal to about half of the U.S. GDP. CLOs and leveraged loans, notably including borrowing to pay dividends to private equity investors, again boomed. The leveraged loans included this borrowing. The CLOs benefitted from the dividends. We reflect that all bubbles implode eventually, and the consequences of the ultimate deflation of the Everything Bubble may be dramatic.

Speaking of repetitive booms and busts, we turn to commercial real estate, a classic area of significant risk to the banking system.

Much of the funding for commercial real estate has historically come from banks; from 1980 to 2020, banks provided approximately 50 percent of the funding for commercial real estate. As of June 30, 2021, commercial real estate loans represented about $2.5 trillion or 23 percent of the banking industry's total loans. The over 800 medium-sized banks,[7] however, had 45 percent of their loans in commercial real estate, while total real estate loans were 70 percent of all their loans.[8]

The risks caused by commercial real estate loans are generally higher for many such banks, which tend to combine high levels of commercial real estate loan exposure with less diversified lending portfolios. Many regional banks and community banks, rather than being called commercial banks, could be more accurately labeled "real estate banks."

Historically, the credit performance of commercial real estate loans has been volatile and these loans have often been a major cause of bank failures. In the hundreds of bank failures between 1980 and 1993, banks that failed had higher concentrations of commercial real estate loans than those that survived. A Government Accountability Office Report concluded that from 2008–11, failures of small and medium-sized banks were largely associated with high concentrations of commercial real estate loans.[9]

The Covid pandemic created unprecedented stress on large sectors of the commercial real estate market. The crisis included shutdowns of many retailers and defaults on shopping mall loans. Businesses across the country adopted work-from-home policies, resulting in many largely empty office buildings. As we write, the long-term impact on the commercial real estate sector remains unclear. Some businesses have mandated that employees return to work full time while others are continuing full or limited work-from-home policies. The emergence and spread of new Covid variants, the Delta and Omicron variants in 2021 and 2022, and unknown others in the future, suggest that commercial real estate may not yet be out of the Covid pandemic woods, even as government rent payment and eviction moratoria and pandemic-related subsidies end. All of this raises the possibility that the large exposure of banks to this sector may result in continuing problems down the line, particularly for regional and community banks, especially if interest rates rise to historically normal levels.

Consumer debt also increased during the recovery and financial market boom. Aggregate household debt increased by $333 billion in the fourth quarter of 2021 over the previous quarter to reach $15.6 trillion.[10] The fourth-quarter number reflected a $1 trillion increase in 2021 and was $1.4 trillion over the year-end 2019 total. The consumer debt included a staggering $1.6 trillion in student loan debt. We take up student loans in Chapter 11.

Reported delinquency rates on household debt are low and declined during the pandemic. This reflected the economic recovery, the low-interest-rate environment, and the government subsidies paid to households resulting from the pandemic, but also, as the Federal Reserve Bank of New York has noted, the reported delinquency rates reflect the requirement of government loan forbearance programs that loans in forbearance with missed payments not be reported as delinquent. To get an accurate picture of loan delinquencies, these loans would have to be included.

We began this chapter with the banks making huge provisions for expected loan losses in 2020. For example, in the panicked second quarter of 2020, the total provision for bank credit losses was $62 billion, an increase of nearly $42 billion, or three times the bank provisions in the second quarter of 2019.[11] As discussed, many banks subsequently reversed these loan loss provisions, bolstering the profits reported at that point. Going forward from early 2022, we have to think about the banking effects of asset price deterioration if or when the Everything Bubble deflates. Setting the level of loss reserves is at least as much art as science and is dependent on forecasts of the economic and financial future. Such forecasts are, needless to say, unreliable and subject to surprises. Like many other things, the wisdom of the banks' decisions to reduce their loan loss reserves will be determined only in light of future events.

The impact of loan loss reserves on the banking sector during the Covid crisis includes the new accounting standard for loan loss provisions that became applicable to all lenders at about the same time as the Covid crisis. This is the Current Expected Credit Losses (CECL) standard, a sharply debated and debatable accounting theory which, as always with complex accounting ideas, leads us to paraphrase Pontius Pilate's question as "What is accounting truth?"

CECL focuses on estimating expected losses over the entire life of a loan, subject to an economic forecast. It replaced an accounting standard that focused on the apparent inability of the borrowers to pay interest and principal and required a management judgment that losses would probably occur. In contrast, CECL requires banks at the time a loan is made to reserve for losses that may occur for macro reasons exogenous to the borrower, including as a result of future financial crises. Therefore, in forecasting losses under CECL, banks must now arguably include the possibility of a future financial crisis in their models.

The combination of looking at losses over a longer term and considering macroeconomic factors that might cause losses meant logically that loan loss provisions were likely to significantly increase as a result of CECL, at least for longer term loans. Naturally, that proved very controversial during the crisis. Regional and community banks and a number of members of Congress argued that CECL, by requiring banks to reserve more for losses when a loan is made, would worsen the financial downturn precipitated by the pandemic and result in banks lending less, just when credit was already constrained. CECL, they argued, would make financial downturns worse and was therefore "procyclical." Others argued that CECL was "countercyclical" because, by boosting bank's loan loss reserves, it would better prepare them to cope with future crises.

As a result of the criticisms, Congress delayed the implementation of CECL (until the earlier of two dates: the end of the national emergency declaration related to the Covid crisis and December 31, 2022).[12] We view this as a sensible action under the crisis circumstances. But many banks, particularly the larger ones, elected to implement CECL in 2020, and this influenced the large loan loss provisions taken in 2020, now viewed in retrospect as excessive.

The CECL debate is in fact about some fundamental banking ideas. It wrestles with the essential concept of credit risk and how to represent it in financial statements. It is best understood in the context of a long-standing dispute, both conceptual and political, between banks and their regulators on one side, and the SEC, as regulator of public accounting and disclosure for investors, on the other side. Many bankers traditionally regarded loan loss reserves the way squirrels view acorns during the autumn. In times of plenty, squirrels like to put away acorns for the hard times of winter. Similarly, when prudent bankers have good years, they wish to increase their provisions for loan losses in anticipation of bad times that they know will come at some point. They know that when the problems eventually occur, it will be better to have a larger loan loss reserve. Bank regulators, seeking to avoid potential bank failures, also prefer robust loan loss reserves.

The SEC's argument is that this distorts reported earnings. Increasing your loan loss provision results in a direct charge to income and thus, in good times, lower reported earnings than the SEC believes were actually earned. It then makes reported earnings higher in bad times, as banks dip into their "cookie jar" of reserves. During the 1990s, SEC officials stressed this problem in a number of public statements and in a well-publicized investigation of SunTrust Bank that resulted in a forced reduction in SunTrust's loan loss reserves.[13] The bank regulators initially sided with the banks in this dispute but eventually knuckled under to the SEC.

In this context, we see CECL as really a victory for the banks. Under CECL, banks have flexibility in developing models that attempt to predict the financial downturns that increase loan losses, and they can thereby reserve more for the ineluctable uncertainty of the financial future. As this book contends, neither the authors, nor banks, nor bank regulators, nor the SEC, nor you, Excellent Reader, can reliably predict when downturns are coming, as we all failed to predict the Covid crisis of 2020. CECL gives bankers flexibility to more prudently build up loan loss reserves under official accounting rules, which they should like.

However, in postponing the mandatory applicability of CECL during the Covid crisis, in our view Congress acted wisely. The implementation of CECL, which is bound to increase bank loan loss reserves, is a prudent direction, consistent with banking tradition; but requiring its introduction in the middle of a financial crisis would have made things worse. The logic of the crisis and the logic of normal times are different with respect to this issue, as in many other ways.

In *Boom and Bust—Financial Cycles and Human Prosperity*, Alex argued that cycles have gone up and down since the seven fat and seven lean years described in the Book of Genesis and are a product of human nature. Prosperity breeds over-optimism and excess, which will be followed by the correction. As Cato the Elder said in ancient Rome, "Most men's spirits are lifted when the times are prosperous, rich and happy, so that their pride and arrogance grow. . . . Adversity chastens them and teaches them what should be done"—until the next enthusiasm, that is.

Perhaps the inevitable banking and financial cycles can be moderated by countercyclical policies. We think it is worth a try. One key countercyclical strategy is to take the inflation of asset prices into account in the management of credit. Thus, lenders would lend less against the current market prices of assets as they increase in a boom to help avoid inflating them into a bubble. This means that if the prices of houses and commercial real estate rapidly rise over their long-term trend, then required down payments would become higher, and loan-to-value ratios become lower, for both kinds of real estate loans. In a very positive step in this direction, the Federal Housing Finance Agency set a countercyclical capital adjustment in the rules it adopted for Fannie Mae and Freddie Mac, which takes effect when house prices are more than five percent above or below their long-term trends. Combined with CECL and bigger loss reserves in good times, such countercyclical adjustments could possibly mitigate the impact of the next crisis.

But during the boom in 2021, the residential mortgage sector was definitely not experiencing a countercyclical policy; indeed, the Federal Reserve was still procyclically stoking house prices with all-time low interest rates and very large purchases of mortgage securities, as we take up next.

CHAPTER 8

The Mortgage Market
Built on a Government Financial Triangle

IN THE WAKE of the Covid financial crisis, the United States experienced runaway house price inflation, which continues as we write, although it will not go on forever. House prices on average were up 19 percent in October 2021 over the year before. From the panic month of March 2020 to October 2021, they increased 27 percent.[1] The median sales price of an existing house in November 2021 was 30 percent higher than it had been in November 2019, before the Covid pandemic. House prices have important financial, economic, and political effects. We showed their rapid inflation in Chapter 5 and repeat it here as Graph 8.1.

In a longer-term perspective, house prices in late 2021 were 48 percent over the memorable peak they reached in 2006, during the frenzy of the infamous Housing Bubble of 1999–2006. When adjusted for consumer price inflation, these late 2021 prices were in real terms 8 percent over the highest point of the previous Bubble and still continued their rapid ascent. Behavioral changes due to the Covid pandemic caused some of these effects. But in financial fundamentals, the prices reflected the exceptionally low interest rates on mortgages engineered by the Federal Reserve. Because houses are generally bought with very high leverage—with mortgage borrowing of 80 percent, or 90 percent or more of the purchase price—the amount of the monthly mortgage payment, and therefore what house price the buyer can afford, greatly

GRAPH 8.1

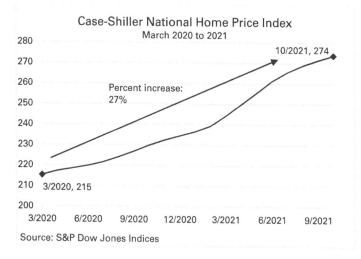

Case-Shiller National Home Price Index
March 2020 to 2021

Percent increase: 27%

10/2021, 274

3/2020, 215

Source: S&P Dow Jones Indices

depends on the level of mortgage interest rates. In general, lower long-term mortgage interest rates mean higher house prices and significantly higher interest rates mean lower house prices.

The American residential mortgage market that finances these inflating house prices is the biggest loan market in the world, with $11.5 trillion in outstanding loans.[2] Alex is fond of reminding his readers that the collateral for these mortgage loans is not the house, but the *price* of the house.

The Government Mortgage Triangle

Housing finance is a highly political market and its finances are thoroughly intertwined with the federal government. It features a triangle of principal government entities: the Government Mortgage Complex, the U.S. Treasury, and the Federal Reserve, which in their huge mortgage finance activities are mutually interdependent.

First, what we call the "Government Mortgage Complex" consists of the government-sponsored and majority government-owned mortgage companies Fannie Mae and Freddie Mac, plus the 100-percent-government-owned agency, Ginnie Mae (which guarantees the mortgage loans of the Federal Housing Administration and the Veterans Administration). Together, these are dominant forces in U.S. housing finance. The risks they take are, in the end, risks to the U. S. Treasury and thus to the taxpayers.

Previously, Fannie and Freddie were ostensibly private corporations with private shareholders—but with government sponsorship, an "implied" government guarantee, and numerous special privileges. Since 2008, they have been operating under federal conservatorship, under the complete control of the government, with their policies dictated by the Federal Housing Finance Agency (FHFA) as Conservator. There have been endless Washington discussions in the past decade about how to return them to private ownership and impose some market discipline on their activities. As we write, the Biden administration has abandoned these efforts, and these two "government-sponsored enterprises" continue to operate as simple arms of the federal government. They are likely to continue to do so for the foreseeable future.

The Government Mortgage Complex guarantees $7.9 trillion of residential mortgages as of late 2021—a remarkable number. That is 69 percent of the total mortgage market. Does it make sense to have 69 percent of the credit risk of the whole mortgage market shifted to the taxpayers? Not to us. How about to you, Thoughtful Reader?

The $7.9 trillion of residential mortgage credit risk guaranteed by the Government Mortgage Complex is shown in Table 8.2.

In addition to residential mortgage credit, these three government organizations together guarantee about $870 billion of

TABLE 8.2
Government Mortgage Complex Guarantees

Fannie Mae	$3.5 trillion
Freddie Mac	2.4
Ginnie Mae	2.0
Total Residential Mortgages Guaranteed	$7.9 trillion

Source: Financial Statements

apartment building ("multifamily") loans, which brings the grand total of their guarantees to $8.8 trillion. Without doubt, they are of major systemic importance because of their huge size, which concentrates mortgage risk on the banks of the Potomac River, and in addition they increase the leverage of the entire housing finance system. The Financial Stability Oversight Council, which we met in Chapter 1, recognized that Fannie and Freddie could pose a risk to U.S. financial stability,[3] but the council has repeatedly refused to take the logical step of formally addressing whether they should be designated as systemically important financial institutions, though it is utterly obvious that they are.[4] Formally facing these undeniable systemic risks was politically inconvenient, and so not done.

This refusal may be viewed as ironically amusing or sadly disillusioning, depending on your point of view, but in any case, it demonstrates again that housing finance is intensely political. About that, no practitioner, regulator, investor, or politician is in doubt.

Alex is the co-author of a 2021 study of the big picture evolution of the banking credit system over the 50 years from 1970 to 2020.[5] The definition of the "banking credit system" is the combination of all banks, big and small, the Government Mortgage Complex, and the Federal Reserve, as one total credit system. Over this half century, the scale of the institutions involved has expanded dramatically, but most notably in the government's mortgage operations.

The Government Mortgage Complex in 1970 was basically a rounding error in the total system, representing $32 billion in assets and 3 percent of the total. By 2020, its assets had grown to $8.3 trillion, or 260 times as large, and it had become 22 percent of the total.

While all U.S. banks grew on average 6.9 percent per year, the Government Mortgage Complex grew 11.8 percent per year, sucking in a greater and greater proportion of the total mortgage credit risk. This was 70 percent faster than the banks and almost twice as fast as the nominal GDP growth rate of 6.1 percent. It is hard or impossible for any private company to compete with these government-guaranteed and government-privileged operations.

The second leg in the government mortgage triangle is the United States Treasury, which is the majority owner of both Fannie and Freddie and effectively guarantees all their obligations. Through clever financial lawyering, the "guarantee" is not a *legal* guarantee, because that would require the honest inclusion of Fannie and Freddie's debt in the calculation of the total U.S. government debt. It will not surprise you that such honest accounting is not politically desired. The same politically undesired accounting result would follow if, in addition to owning 100 percent of Fannie and Freddie's senior preferred stock, the Treasury owned 80 percent of their common stock—that is why the Treasury instead owns warrants for 79.9 percent of that common stock. For historical perspective, getting Fannie Mae's debt *off* the government's books was the principal reason for restructuring it into a "government-sponsored enterprise" in 1968.

Everybody involved, especially the holders of Fannie and Freddie's debt and mortgage-backed securities, knows that the Treasury's involvement with Fannie and Freddie really is a guarantee. Everybody involved knows that, through the Treasury, the taxpayers really are on the hook for Fannie and Freddie. In addition, the Treasury and the taxpayers are explicitly and fully on the hook for Ginnie's obligations. The Treasury is thus deeply involved in the mortgage business.

The third leg of the government triangle is the Federal Reserve, which has become a huge funder of mortgage securities. These Federal Reserve holdings are limited to those guaranteed by Fannie, Freddie, or Ginnie, but their guarantees in turn are only credible because they are backed by the U.S. Treasury. At the same time, an essential element in the credit of the Treasury itself is the willingness of the Federal Reserve to buy government debt in any amount by printing money. At the end of 2021, the Federal Reserve owned $5.7 trillion of direct Treasury debt in addition to its $2.6 trillion of mortgages, all ultimately guaranteed by the Treasury. The Treasury and the Federal Reserve thus mutually support each other, and both support the Government Mortgage Complex.

Faced with the post-Covid panic extreme house price inflation, the Federal Reserve, unbelievably to us, kept on stimulating the market by buying ever more mortgage securities. It continued throughout 2021 to be the price-setting marginal buyer or Big Bid for mortgage securities, expanding its mortgage portfolio with one hand, and printing money with the other. These purchases, at the rate of tens of billions of dollars a month, kept mortgage interest rates abnormally low and stoked the house price inflation. While making existing homeowners feel richer, it made it harder and harder for new families, notably many low-income families, to afford a house. A 2021 *Wall Street Journal* opinion piece was entitled "How the Fed Rigs the Bond Market"—it also rigged the mortgage market.

In December 2006 (just before the last crisis), the total assets of the Federal Reserve were $875 billion, and total mortgage investments were zero. At the end of 2021, the Federal Reserve owned on its balance sheet $2.6 trillion in mortgage securities. That means about 23 percent of all the residential mortgages in the entire country resided in the central bank. The Federal Reserve thereby earned the remarkable status of having become by far the largest savings and loan institution in the world. The path of its mortgage portfolio from zero to $2.6 trillion, with the acceleration in 2020–21, is shown in Graph 8.3.

Like the historical savings and loan industry, which collapsed in the 1980s, the Federal Reserve owns long-term mortgages, with interest rates that are fixed for 15 to 30 years, and it neither marks its investments to market in its financial statements nor hedges its extremely large interest rate risk. It reports its mortgage securities at par value and separately reported $70 billion of unamortized net premium paid on mortgage securities, which is an additional investment in them.

The Federal Reserve's $2.6 trillion in mortgage securities is double the level of March 2020, but more to the point, it is infinitely greater than the zero it always was up until 2006. From the

GRAPH 8.3

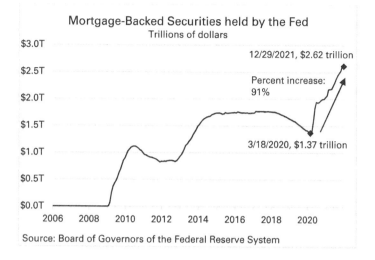

Mortgage-Backed Securities held by the Fed
Trillions of dollars

12/29/2021, $2.62 trillion

Percent increase:
91%

3/18/2020, $1.37 trillion

Source: Board of Governors of the Federal Reserve System

founding of the Federal Reserve in 1913 to 2006, the number of mortgage assets it owned had always been zero. That was normal. What is normal now?

In the 1960s, the Congress pressured the Federal Reserve to support the housing market by buying the debt issues (not mortgage securities) of Fannie Mae and other federal agencies involved with housing. The Federal Reserve of the time resisted. Chairman William McChesney Martin testified that such an idea would "violate a fundamental principle of sound monetary policy, in that it would attempt to use the credit-creating powers of the central bank to subsidize programs benefiting special sectors of the economy."

That seems to us exactly the right principle for normal times. In the last two crises, the Federal Reserve has decided to implement the opposite of Martin's principle, that is, precisely "to use the credit-creating powers of the central bank to subsidize" a particular sector of the economy, and a highly political one: housing finance. When the crises are over, and the interventions have become distortions, what then? Can we now even imagine a Federal Reserve that owns zero mortgages? At this point, can the Federal Reserve itself imagine that?

Whether one considers the Federal Reserve's subsidizing mortgages by monetization and thereby inflating the price of houses as crisis management, or longer-term distortion, or both, it is without doubt a major change in American central banking theory and practice. It was an emergency action in 2009 and again in 2020. But should it be permanent as a "new normal," or temporary? If temporary, how long should it continue? How long is temporary?

In November and December 2021, the Federal Reserve announced that it would "taper" (as it says) its purchases of mortgage securities, as well as of Treasury bonds. It planned to slow down the increase in its portfolio in stepwise fashion until the net increase would reach zero in March 2022. Until then, it would still be buying. It also announced it would have discussions of whether in the future its balance sheet might be reduced. If the Federal Reserve did actually let its mortgage portfolio run off, it would take a long time—perhaps lasting into the next financial crisis. Will the Federal Reserve ever actually sell a single mortgage security? We believe nobody knows, including the Federal Reserve.

A reasonable argument is that the Federal Financial Triangle should be consolidated into a single set of books, and all the obscuring transactions among the Treasury, the Federal Reserve, and Fannie and Freddie become consolidating eliminations. With these consolidated books, we would then see clearly what has been happening net: namely, the government printing money to buy mortgage loans.

In a long-term view, given all the government intervention and its subsidization of mortgage credit directed at home ownership, it is ironic that the U.S. home ownership rate has been more or less flat for the last half century. The percent of all households owning their own home was 65.4 percent in the third quarter of 2021. Fifty years before, at the end of 1971, it was 64.5 percent—less than a percentage point difference. The ratio has varied from 69 percent on the high side in the infamous 2000s Housing Bubble, to a low of 63 percent in the wake of that Bubble's implosion, but the trend in the American home ownership rate is essentially sideways. This is in spite of five decades of massive government interventions of many kinds in housing finance, all meant to increase home ownership.[6]

We believe it probable that much of the effect of the government interventions unintentionally went into increasing the price of houses. As distinguished housing economist Ernest Fisher pointed out in 1975:

> The tendency for costs and prices to absorb the amounts made available to prospective purchasers or renters has plagued government programs since . . . 1934. Close examination of these tendencies indicates that promises of extending the loan-to-value ratio of the mortgage and extending its term so as to make home purchase "possible for lower income prospective purchasers" may bring greater profits to and wages to builders, building suppliers, and building labor rather than assisting lower-income households.[7]

That subsidies and expanding credit turn into higher prices is a lesson the government never learns, although we can be sure that the housing industry understands it perfectly, consistent with Fisher's observation.

A Bigger Punch Bowl

Late in 2021, the Federal Housing Finance Agency once again increased by regulation the size of the mortgage loans Fannie and Freddie can buy (known as the "conforming loan limit") to $970,800 in "high cost areas." With a standard 20-percent down payment, that means Fannie and Freddie will be financing loans for the purchase of houses costing up to $1,213,500. In other words, Fannie and Freddie will put taxpayers on the hook for the risks of financing $1.2 million houses.

Similarly, and perhaps more surprising, the Federal Housing Administration (FHA), which is the government's sub-prime mortgage lender, will be subsidizing the purchase of houses costing up to $1,011,250. That amount is the price of a house bought with the corresponding FHA "high cost" limit of $970,800 and a typical FHA down payment of only 4 percent, thus putting taxpayers on the hook for loans on more million dollar houses.

Average Americans who own ordinary houses may think it makes no sense for the government to support people who buy, lenders that lend on, and builders that build, such $1.2 million or $1 million houses—not to mention the Wall Street firms that make money on the resulting government-backed mortgage securities. The average Americans are right.

At the same time, the regular Fannie and Freddie loan limit was raised to $647,200, which, with a 20-percent down payment, means a house costing $809,000. In sharp contrast, the median U.S. house price for houses sold in mid-2021 was $310,000. A house selling for $809,000 is in the top 7 percent in the country. One selling for $1.2 million is in the top 3 percent. For FHA loans, the regular limit correspondingly became $420,680, or, with a 4-percent down payment, a house costing $438,000—41 percent above the national median sales price.

Of course, Fannie, Freddie, and the FHA have a natural internal desire to grow ever bigger, and of course those who benefit from the subsidies they convey want more of them. In addition to increasing the taxpayers' mortgage risk, expanding the size of these government-supported loans creates procyclical upward pressure on house prices.[8]

By pushing more government credit at high-priced houses, and at houses in general, Fannie; Freddie; their government conservator, the FHFA; and their sister agencies, the FHA and Ginnie Mae, feed the runaway house price inflation instead of acting to moderate it, as a countercyclical policy would do. Procyclical policies, by definition, make financial cycles worse.

The contrasting policy, a countercyclical objective, was memorably expressed by William McChesney Martin, who was the longest-ever-serving Chairman of the Federal Reserve Board, in office from 1951 to 1970, under five U.S. presidents. Martin gave us the most famous of all central banking metaphors: The Federal Reserve, he said in 1955, "is in the position of the chaperone who has ordered the punch bowl removed just when the party was really warming up."

In 2021, long after the housing party was not only warmed up, but had grown tipsy, the Federal Reserve, instead of removing the punch bowl, was spiking the punch. Meanwhile, the Government Mortgage Complex kept increasing the leverage of the mortgage system, and late in the evening, the FHFA and FHA, by upping the loan sizes, brought in a bigger punch bowl.

Of course, removing the punch bowl is easier said than done. As celebrated Federal Reserve Chairman Paul Volcker, who served from 1979 to 1987, pointed out in his autobiography, "The hard fact of life is that few hosts want to end the party prematurely. They wait too long and when the risks are evident the real damage is done. Central bankers are the hosts at the economic party."[9]

When the party turns into a crisis, emergency actions need to be taken; their risks and unintended consequences will be accepted because surviving the crisis becomes the paramount priority. But when do those emergency actions get turned off? This is the Cincinnatian Problem, as discussed further in Chapter 12.

For normal times, when the financial system is not in crisis, we believe a robust mortgage finance market needs less taxpayer subsidy and less government and central bank distortion, not more. We should not continue on the path of making the Government Mortgage Complex, with its massive support from the Federal Reserve and the Treasury, even more massive than the combined $8 trillion it already is as we write. Its taxpayer-guaranteed, subsidized, market-distorting activities should not become even more dominant in mortgage finance than they already are.

In short, when considering the Government Mortgage Complex, especially Fannie and Freddie, one must necessarily ask: Should it get bigger or smaller? We vote for smaller.

Mortgage Servicing in the Covid Crisis

A particular concern among officials at the Treasury in 2020 was the risk to the orderly issuance and servicing of mortgages during the crisis. The difficulty was caused by a shift in the nature of the entities that originate and service mortgage loans from depository institutions to nonbank mortgage companies. By 2020, approximately 60 percent of residential mortgages were originated by nonbank companies, compared to approximately 30 percent before 2008, and more than half of agency-guaranteed residential mortgages were serviced by nonbanks.[10] This reflected in part the regulatory changes made in response to the 2007–09 crisis, which disincentivized banks from being in the residential mortgage business. Nonbank mortgage companies, which were not subject to these regulatory requirements, moved in to fill the vacuum.

These nonbank mortgage originators and servicers were and are dependent for their liquidity on the capital markets and bank warehouse lines of credit, sources of funding that can dry up in financial crises, with catastrophic consequences for the entities involved. For example, almost every REIT that originated mortgages failed during the 2007–09 crisis.

A worrisome systemic problem arose in 2020 because mortgage servicers are contractually required to advance principal and interest payments to the holders of mortgage-backed securities, as well as property tax payments to local governments, even if they themselves do not receive any payments from the mortgage borrowers. In addition, while nonbank mortgage servicers are required to comply with the capital and liquidity requirements contained in their servicing contracts with Fannie, Freddie, and Ginnie, these requirements are nowhere near as strong as the standards applied to banks. Nonbank mortgage servicers are typically required to have state lending licenses, but the states generally have not imposed serious capital or liquidity requirements on these lenders either.

During the Covid crisis, the mortgage moratoria established by the CARES Act and related actions that allowed the deferral of mortgage payments thus unintentionally placed added stress upon the liquidity of the mortgage servicing system. In the spring of 2020, the mortgage bankers and the Treasury feared that the mortgage servicers' being required to make cash payments of principal, interest, and taxes, when they were in fact not receiving payments from the borrowers to fund them, would result in a liquidity crisis and servicer insolvencies. This, in turn, could lead to an inability to have mortgages serviced and a breakdown in mortgage origination—a threatening disruption to the housing market.

We believe that had this occurred, since the crisis brought government bailouts wherever they were needed, the Federal Reserve, with Treasury approval, would rapidly have set up yet another emergency credit program to finance the nonbank mortgage servicing industry.

As it was, according to one mortgage company CEO quoted in the *Wall Street Journal*, "The Federal Reserve, which kept lending and helped convince many banks to go easy on struggling mortgage finance companies, was the main reason the industry survived."[11]

To mitigate the mortgage companies' pressing liquidity risk, Ginnie Mae established backstop financing for its servicers. Fannie Mae and Freddie Mac agreed to limit to four months the exposure of the servicers for advancing cash on the mortgage loans which were not paying. But what really saved the nonbank servicing sector was an effective bailout by the Federal Reserve that, by imposing historically low mortgage interest rates, fueled a massive refinancing boom in residential mortgages. When a mortgage is refinanced, the original mortgage loan is paid off and the proceeds are initially paid to the mortgage servicer for eventual payment to mortgage bondholders. The servicers generally can keep those proceeds for about a month before passing them on, and it was this cash, replenished each month by further refinancings, that enabled nonbank mortgage servicers to remain liquid and survive the pandemic crisis. The way this solution to the nonbank mortgage servicer issue developed was yet another surprise.

As a result of this scare, and with the support of FSOC, the Conference of State Bank Supervisors proposed regulatory standards for state regulators to adopt, that would, among other things, require all state-licensed mortgage servicers to comply with the capital and liquidity requirements that Fannie and Freddie impose by contract on their servicers, but still stronger capital and liquidity standards may be needed. The years-long process for each state to enact such requirements may be overtaken by the next financial crisis before it is complete.

The financial model followed by nonbank mortgage servicers leaves them vulnerable to distress in a financial crisis. They were lucky to have been saved by the refinancing boom in 2020; they may not always be so lucky.

The related world of REITs demonstrates how another federally favored type of entity has added instability to the mortgage markets. REITs, or real estate investment trusts, are entities created by law in 1960 to allow shareholders to own interests in real estate in a tax-advantaged way. Unlike regular corporations that pay tax at the corporate level and whose shareholders pay a second tax when they receive dividends, REITs pay no entity-level corporate income tax. Avoiding an entity-level tax makes REITs more profitable than ordinary corporations, everything else being equal. For this reason, many nonbank mortgage lenders, who are often mortgage servicers as well, are organized as REITs. Yet REITs are ill-suited to be lenders in a cyclical market because they cannot build up retained earnings in the usual corporate way. They are required to pay out dividends of at least 90 percent of their taxable income to their shareholders each year, with most REITs paying out an even higher percentage. Indeed, in order to maintain attractive yields, most mortgage REITs aim to pay dividends of almost 100 percent of their net income. This strictly limits the amount they are able to retain as a capital cushion to apply against loan losses when the market turns down or crashes. Contrast this with banks, which are required to retain significant amounts of capital buffer. In 1999 the REIT law was amended to enable REITs to own taxable subsidiaries where capital could be stored. However, since REITs compete in the investment marketplace in large part by the size of their dividends, mortgage lenders organized as REITs failed to accumulate much capital in their taxable REIT subsidiaries, choosing to use their earnings to pay dividends instead. A mortgage REIT liquidity crisis occurred as part of the Great Recession of 2007–09 and many of these entities failed. In the Covid crisis, refinancings provided liquidity, as we have seen, and house prices rose rather than declined, so these failures were not replicated. Nonetheless, REITs that originate and service mortgages remain vulnerable to future downturns largely because of the unintended consequences of a federal policy designed to stimulate the real estate markets by giving them a tax benefit.

If Mortgage Interest Rates Go Back to Normal, What Then?

A central question for the future of housing finance is what will happen assuming that the Federal Reserve's crisis-induced buying binge of mortgage securities and Treasury bonds does indeed end and its Big Bid for these securities goes away. Even if we do not return to a Federal Reserve that owns zero mortgage investments, its share of the market would be declining. Perhaps even its overall securities portfolio would decline; the Federal Reserve publicly announced in January 2022 that it was discussing a reduction in this portfolio. This is sometimes called "Quantitative Tightening" or QT, as the opposite of QE. In that case, long-term interest rates in general, and mortgage interest rates in particular, will rise—as they have already been rising in early 2022 as we write. How high will they rise?

Let us guess what a normal mortgage interest rate might be with true market rates—meaning, with no Federal Reserve intervention. Suppose we have an expected inflation rate of 3 percent—low, compared to current inflation as we write. Once the Federal Reserve stops being the price-setting Big Buyer for bonds, let us say a more normal yield on the 10-year Treasury note is 1½ percent over inflation, and the 30-year mortgage interest rate is 1½ percent or more over the 10-year Treasury rate. That adds up to a mortgage rate of at least 6 percent. If we start instead with the endlessly discussed Federal Reserve "target" inflation of 2 percent, the estimated mortgage interest rate would be 5 percent. Historically, the 30-year mortgage rate from 1972 to 2009 was always over 5 percent and usually over 6 percent (it got as high as 16 percent in 1981).

Now let us ask: What would mortgage interest rates of 5 percent or 6 percent or more do to current house prices? Compared to a typical Covid-time mortgage rate of 3 percent, the dollars of interest you would have to pay on your mortgage, all else being equal, would go up by 67 percent to 100 percent or more. This would mean that for many potential house buyers, the former house price would become unaffordable. To keep their mortgage payments the same as with the former 3 percent interest, the price they could pay for a house would be significantly lower.

If, or when, the latest house price bubble starts to deflate, the Federal Reserve could intervene once again to prop house prices up. But since this would make its pressing problems with overall inflation worse, would it? The Government Mortgage Complex could and probably would lower credit standards so it could make more loans with higher leverage. Would such actions be enough to offset the inexorable impact of higher mortgage interest rates on house prices? Our guess is No, and that if mortgage interest rates become normalized, this most recent great house price inflation will end with prices falling.

Looking back from where you are, Esteemed Reader, you will know what happened. Did we get it right or were we surprised again?

CHAPTER 9

Municipal Debt in Covid Times

THE COVID PANIC roiled the municipal debt market as it did other financial markets. In early 2020, before the pandemic, the municipal bond market was strong, with municipal bond funds having received net inflows of $93 billion in 2019, as compared with $4.2 billion in 2018. State and local tax revenues, the sources of repayment for municipal debt, had increased. Municipal bond ratings were firm. All of that changed in the panic: investors withdrew $45 billion from municipal bond funds in the flight to cash. Municipal bond issuance fell 53 percent in March 2020 from the prior month, retail demand for municipal bonds plummeted, the market ceased to function efficiently, and traders had difficulty determining prices. One recurring lesson of financial crises is: Where there is no market, there is no market price.

In this chapter, we review the impact of the Covid crisis on the municipal bond market and the market's subsequent recovery, and we consider a key systemic problem that will mark its future, with or without further Covid challenges.

During the height of the Covid panic, from mid-March through April 2020, a rare phenomenon marked the municipal debt market. Municipal securities generally have lower yields than Treasury securities, because their interest is exempt from federal income tax. Using round numbers, a 3-percent tax-exempt yield is worth the same as a 5-percent taxable yield to an investor with a 40-percent marginal income tax rate. There is greater credit risk in municipal securities than in Treasuries, but municipal defaults are relatively infrequent and, while riskier than Treasuries, highly rated municipal securities are deemed safe by investors. There is less active trading and less liquidity in municipals than Treasuries. But the tax advantage outweighs the spread demanded for credit risk and less liquidity, so the overall yield required by investors is generally lower.

In the panic, however, this relationship inverted and municipal bond tax-exempt yields suddenly exceeded taxable Treasury yields significantly. The remarkable disruption in this yield relationship is shown in Graph 9.1.

Graph 9.2 shows another way of expressing this: the ratio of the yields of 10-year AAA-rated general obligation municipal bonds, the safest kind of municipal securities, divided by the 10-year Treasury note. This ratio was about 79 percent at the end of 2019. In the panic, it soared to 313 percent. The 10-year historical average for this ratio is 96 percent. By September 2020, this ratio of municipal bond to Treasury yields had come back to 121 percent, and by September 2021 to 71 percent, and a normal relationship had returned.

GRAPH 9.1

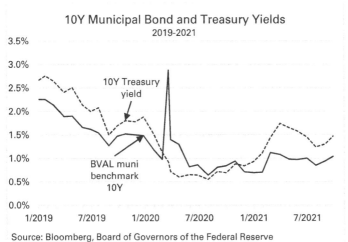

10Y Municipal Bond and Treasury Yields
2019-2021

Source: Bloomberg, Board of Governors of the Federal Reserve

GRAPH 9.1

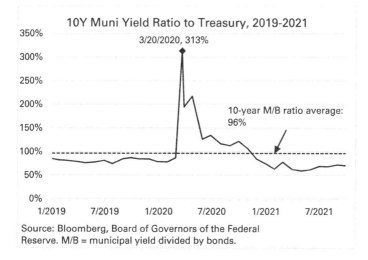

10Y Muni Yield Ratio to Treasury, 2019-2021

Source: Bloomberg, Board of Governors of the Federal
Reserve. M/B = municipal yield divided by bonds.

In retrospect, the sudden spike in municipal yields created an attractive buying opportunity for those able to overcome the prevailing fear, as also happened in other markets. But don't allow yourself to forget, Reflective Reader, the intense uncertainty and the frightening possibilities of the future for investors trying to look forward from that time. Our emotions, unlike theirs, are calmed by looking backward at what actually happened.

Investors were also worried because the pandemic had hurt state and local tax revenues. The mandated pandemic lockdowns caused revenue from income taxes, sales taxes, and business taxes to drop. Revenue from projects funded by municipal debt, such as toll roads, stadiums, and airports, also declined as their use was dramatically cut by the lockdowns.

There are two basic types of municipal debt. General obligation bonds are backed by a jurisdiction's full faith and credit, including all of its revenue from taxes and other sources. Revenue bonds fund specific projects such as airports, stadiums, college dormitories, or toll roads, and are repaid only from revenue generated by the specific project they were issued to fund. Defaults on general obligation bonds are rare, but do happen, as in the very large insolvencies of Detroit and Puerto Rico that marked the decade of the 2010s. Municipalities and states can increase taxes to avoid default on general obligation bonds, but revenue bonds depend on the success of a specific project, so expected declines in revenues from the project can lead to bond defaults. Nobody in early 2020 knew how widespread the pandemic would become, how deadly it would be, how long the lockdowns would last, or how many revenue bond-financed projects might fail.

At the same time that the pandemic was causing state and municipal revenues to fall, it was also causing their expenses to rise. Health care expenses went up as states and localities cared for Covid patients hospitalized in systems they ran. Education expenses also increased as new ventilation and cleaning requirements, as well as additional requirements for space as teachers and students were required to socially distance, increased the costs of running schools, while many schools closed to prevent the spread of Covid and had to establish new virtual teaching systems.

Some municipalities tried to meet the crisis by cutting costs, including by laying off workers. But many localities and states are stuck with high fixed costs to fund the very expensive public employee pension plans they are left with as a result of often bad bargains made with politically powerful public employee unions. On average, these plans are substantially underfunded. This means that states and localities must make large periodic payments to fund their pension plans. Not surprisingly, during the pandemic, some states and localities sought to postpone these payments.

The panicked tenor of the early 2020 municipal bond market changed dramatically on April 9, 2020, when the Federal Reserve used its elastic currency powers to support the market's investors and borrowers, announcing the creation of its Municipal Liquidity Facility (MLF) to purchase up to $500 billion in debt from eligible state and local issuers. In August, the Federal Reserve extended this program to year-end 2020. Even though only two very financially troubled entities, the State of Illinois and the New York Metropolitan Transportation Authority, actually borrowed from the MLF, the announcement of the program helped calm fear and restore investor confidence: the Federal Reserve cavalry had arrived. In short order, pricing stabilized in the municipal markets, municipal bond issuance increased, and new money once again flowed into municipal bond funds. Between May and September 2020, $43 billion was invested in these funds.

As discussed in Chapter 3, the principal reason the Federal Reserve was created in 1913 was to act as an emergency lender in panicked times. Once yet again in 2020, experience proved that this is something the Federal Reserve is good at, and this time the emergency lending included the municipal bond market.

On top of that, the emergency American Rescue Plan Act of March 2021 allocated $350 billion to state and local governments. This federal government bailout significantly shored up municipal borrowers and investors and the municipal bond market.

In the history of this market, interestingly, defaults by U.S. states on their bonds did occur a number of times in the 19th century (not counting the nonpayment of their debt by Confederate states after the Civil War), and some state debt was actually repudiated. The bondholders of the day implored the federal government to bail them out, but the government refused. In the 20th century, the State of Arkansas defaulted during the Great Depression, but later paid.

Defaults by states now seem unlikely, because states generally have the power to increase their revenues by raising taxes, although they must trade off the risk of driving away businesses and population by raising taxes to pay for the past deficits that caused the debt. Most states derive most of their tax revenues from individual income taxes and sales taxes. The pandemic caused threatening declines in state tax revenues, but by early 2021, total state tax receipts were about the same in the twelve months from March 2020 through February 2021 as they were for the same months a year prior.[1] With time, the overall state budget situation became much more optimistic. By July 2021, ABC News could run a story with the headline, "States, cities that expected to go bankrupt from pandemic now seeing cash surplus." In January 2022, the *Wall Street Journal* wrote that "States are Swimming in Cash Thanks to Booming Tax Revenue and Federal Aid," although one analyst cautioned, "these surpluses are likely temporary."[2] Again, there were two surprises: first, the crisis and the fear it engendered; and second, the extent of the subsequent improvement, which reflected the overall economic recovery plus federal bailout money printed up by the Federal Reserve.

Should there ever again be a default by a U.S. state, the consequences are unforeseeable. States, being sovereign entities under the Constitution, cannot declare bankruptcy under the U.S. Bankruptcy Code, which would entail putting themselves under the direction of a federal judge, nor can they be petitioned into bankruptcy by their creditors. Either would be inconsistent with the federal structure created by the Constitution.

The situation is further complicated by the Eleventh Amendment to the Constitution, ratified in 1795—the first amendment after the original Bill of Rights. Under its provisions, bondholders cannot sue a state in federal court to enforce their rights as creditors. Says the very little-known Eleventh Amendment:

> The Judicial power of the United States shall not be construed to extend to any suit in law or equity, commenced or prosecuted against one of the United States by Citizens of another State, or by Citizens or Subjects of any Foreign State.

So should a state be unable to pay its debt in full, for whatever reason, it would surely be messy and its bondholders would experience the time-proven risks of lending to sovereign borrowers. We note that across the world from 1800 to 2020, there have been more than 250 defaults by sovereign governments on their debt. Six of these defaults were in 2020,[3] and 146 governments have defaulted since 1960.[4]

As we write, a number of states are still under some degree of financial pressure, particularly as a result of unaffordable public pension plans. Although virtually every state has a balanced budget provision in its state constitution, pension fund deficits, which have become massive, escape this intended discipline.

The balanced budget provisions generally only deal with a state's operating budget and not its capital budget, and they do not prevent a state from mortgaging its future with pension promises it can't afford.

Illinois is the worst example of this type of excess. Illinois reported that the amount of unfunded liabilities in its state pension plans rose to a staggering $144 billion as of 2020, according to the state's own estimate, and the state had run budget deficits for 20 years in a row. As a result of Illinois' impecuniousness, its bonds had received numerous rating agency downgrades to one notch above junk status. Illinois' need for cash to fund its deficits led it, as noted above, to become one of only two entities to borrow from the Federal Reserve's Municipal Liquidity Facility. For the Federal Reserve to be a "lender of last resort" to a state was an unprecedented event and displayed the depth of Illinois' financial woes.

The $1.9 trillion American Rescue Plan, which became law in the early days of the Biden administration, when the economic recovery was already well-established, allocated about $8 billion to Illinois, thereby providing the state with a substantial federal bailout. That, and a new budget reflecting the economic recovery, led Moody's to upgrade Illinois' bond grading to two notches above junk status in June 2021. This was Illinois' first ratings upgrade in 23 years, but it still left it with the lowest credit rating of any state.[5] Moody's tempered its opinion by also writing that the size of Illinois' pension debt is "unusually large," and "as federal support dissipates," the debt could "exert growing pressure" on the state without new revenues, spending reductions, or actual structural reforms.[6] In other words, American taxpayers subsidized Illinois, but even an $8 billion bailout does not begin to put a dent into the state's $144 billion unfunded pension burden (which, as we discuss in Chapter 10, may be a low estimate).

The only long-term hope for Illinois, and for the risk its massive pension fund deficits pose to its bondholders, would necessarily involve structural changes to the state pension system, or, alternatively, very large tax increases and cutbacks in services to pay for past mistakes. Or a bigger federal bailout.

The inability to change the status quo is exacerbated in Illinois and other states by requirements in state constitutions that treat pension plans as vested contracts and prevent the state from modifying pension arrangements. Structural reforms may therefore require amendments to the state constitution, which are very difficult to implement. In any event, such reform is forcefully resisted by politically powerful public employee unions.

Municipalities, in contrast to states, depend primarily on property taxes for revenues. By late 2021, the Everything Bubble included a dramatic increase in residential housing prices, which increased property tax revenues—at least until the bubble bursts. According to the United States Census Bureau, in the third quarter of 2020, state and local property tax revenue had already increased 5.6 percent over the same quarter in 2019.[7] Some municipalities, such as New York City, are heavily dependent on sales tax revenues, and those revenues declined sharply in 2020[8] before recovering in 2021 and running above previous projections.[9]

Municipalities, if authorized by their state, unlike the states themselves, may declare bankruptcy under Chapter 9 of the United States Bankruptcy Code. Four municipalities filed for Chapter 9 bankruptcy in 2019, two in 2020, and three in 2021.[10] Meanwhile, 82 municipal bond issuers totaling $5.8 billion of principal defaulted in 2020, making it the worst year for municipal bond defaults since 2012. Virtually all of these defaults were in revenue bonds backed by projects in sectors of the economy most severely impacted by Covid. More than a third of the defaults were by issuers in the retirement sector, which includes nursing homes, a sector particularly hard hit by Covid, given the high incidence of illness and death among older people. Most of these defaults also occurred in revenue bonds that were initially unrated by a credit rating agency.[11] An additional 60 municipal bond issuers defaulted in 2021, MarketWatch estimated, with senior living facility bonds accounting for the greatest number of defaults, followed by charter schools.[12]

Not surprisingly, investors' search and reach for yield at a time when the Federal Reserve has kept interest rates near zero accelerated the issuance of high-yield municipal bonds. High-yield municipal bonds predominate in sectors perceived as high risk, such as schools, hospitals, toll roads, nursing homes, and senior and student housing. Future default rates in this sector are likely to be influenced by how new virus variants, like the Covid Delta or Omicron variants, may spread, and whether the changes in the way we live our lives caused by the pandemic continue.

While the municipal securities market not only recovered but had its own post-Covid crisis bull market, weaknesses continue in the area of high-yield municipal bonds that heavily fund market sectors impacted adversely by the pandemic, and in those state and local issuers that are burdened by unsupportable debt levels arising from underfunded public employee pension plans that they could never realistically have afforded.

Among major cities, Chicago appears to be in particular financial trouble. It faced a $1.2 billion budget deficit in 2021 and in mid-2021 projected a $733 million shortfall for 2022. This budget gap was closed principally with $385 million in special federal support under the American Rescue Plan. "When the federal money is gone, Chicago will be left with higher debt and funding issues," said the City Council's Office of Financial Analysis.[13] Most financially daunting of all, Chicago faces $33 billion in unfunded pension liabilities.[14] This also may be an understatement, as we discuss in Chapter 10.

A particularly instructive example of what can go wrong in the municipal bond market is the Puerto Rican debt crisis. Puerto Rico is a U.S. territory and was a major issuer of municipal debt. Since the Jones-Shafroth Act of 1917, Puerto Rican bonds have been exempt not only from federal income taxes, like other municipal bonds, but also from all state and local income taxes. This special privilege made them extremely attractive to taxable U.S. investors. No U.S. states or municipalities get this special triple tax-exempt advantage. Even if this statutory subsidy might have made sense in 1917, the history of Puerto Rican debt suggests to us that 105 years later it no longer does, and it should be repealed.

Puerto Rico took advantage of this especially privileged tax status to issue debt to fund recurring operating budget deficits for a decade, and then borrowed more to service the existing debt, often at higher interest rates. By 2014, Puerto Rico's debt had grown to $71 billion, and three bond rating agencies had downgraded its bonds to junk status.

In 2016, faced with the Puerto Rican government's obvious and admitted insolvency, combined with its legal inability to declare bankruptcy, Congress enacted the Puerto Rico Oversight, Management, and Economic Stability Act (PROMESA). This act created the Financial Oversight and Management Board for Puerto Rico (Oversight Board) and a federal court-supervised process for reorganizing Puerto Rico's debt, modeled on Chapter 9 municipal bankruptcy. The framework established by PROMESA was used beginning in 2016 to address reorganization of the island's swollen debt.

Puerto Rico had $74 billion in bond debt and $49 billion in unfunded pension liabilities as of May 2017.[15] Pension funds compete with bondholders for the available assets of an insolvent borrower. Thus, the total debt under negotiation was $123 billion—more than six times the total debt of Detroit, the previous record municipal insolvency.

For decades, Puerto Rico benefited from special U.S. tax subsidies that encouraged companies to locate businesses on the island, but these tax subsidies were phased out between 1996 and 2006. Businesses with no reason to stay other than the tax subsidies left, which reduced Puerto Rico's tax revenues. Puerto Rico then ran budget deficits every year, funded by issuing more and more debt. The *New York Times* blamed Puerto Rico's debt crisis on "a failing economy and an inefficient government that has spent more than it has taken in for years, often borrowing to close the gap."[16] Others blamed "decades of mismanagement, corruption and excessive borrowing to balance budgets."[17] A day of reckoning was inevitable and indeed arrived.

In February 2020, the Oversight Board filed a plan with the court to restructure debt, pension liabilities, and other claims against Puerto Rico and its governmental entities. Although the plan would have greatly reduced Puerto Rico's overall debt, the Governor of Puerto Rico opposed it because it would reduce some pensions.[18] The Oversight Board forged ahead; in November 2021, it submitted a revised plan.

In January 2022, a federal court approved a final settlement in which overall debts would be written down by $30 billion and the government of Puerto Rico would leave its equivalent of bankruptcy, concluding the largest municipal debt reorganization in history. Pension payments were untouched, demonstrating again that pensions are de facto senior to bonds. Getting to this settlement is a major achievement of the Oversight Board, which, under its charter in PROMESA, remains in existence until Puerto Rico has four consecutive years of balanced budgets. Will that be achieved?

Puerto Rico's poverty rate is estimated to be about twice that of Mississippi, the poorest state. In the Covid economic contraction in June 2020, Puerto Rico's unemployment rate reached 23 percent, the highest in the United States. In mid-2021 it was still high, at about 8 percent. Moreover, the labor participation rate is extremely low at only 42 percent in mid-2021. Even before the pandemic, Puerto Rico's average household income was approximately one-third of the U.S. average, and its unemployment rate was more than twice the U.S. average at 8 percent.[19] The causes of these dismal economic numbers have resulted in an exodus from the island, which has left fewer taxpayers to share the burden of Puerto Rico's indebtedness, even after the creditors take their losses. According to the Council on Foreign Relations, of all living Puerto Ricans born on the island, more than half have moved elsewhere—a depressing statistic.[20]

The recipe for financial disaster in Puerto Rico was a mix of unaffordable government transfer payments, inefficient and often-corrupt government, continuous borrowing to fund continuous operating deficits, and a large and almost entirely unfunded public pension liability. It is not surprising that this led to the exodus of people to places where they can get a job and have less of a debt burden to fund through their future taxes. In a more extreme form, this is the same mix that we have seen in Illinois, where the population also declined—by 80,000 in 2020, the seventh year in a row of population loss.

The problems faced by Puerto Rico and Illinois and their creditors were exacerbated by the Covid crisis but reflect underlying fundamental problems which will continue. Of course, Puerto Rico and Illinois are not the only places where unfunded public employee pension liabilities are a problem, even though Illinois has the worst record of any state in this regard. Other states, including Connecticut, Rhode Island, and California, also face this problem, as do many municipalities, including Chicago, Philadelphia, New York City, and San Jose, of which Chicago is the worst. While the Municipal Liquidity Facility and the American Rescue Plan Act infused states and localities with large amounts of newly printed federal money to help them meet their budgets and pay their debts in the short term, the aggregate amount of pension funding shortfalls dwarfs the amount of federal aid.

Without important reforms to many public pension plans, they will continue to pose large risks to the future of municipal finance, even while the memories of the Covid panic in the municipal bond market fade away.

CHAPTER 10

Pension Funds

Some Dubious Promises

We have just considered the financial drag on municipal finances from troubled public pension funds, noting particularly those of Illinois and Puerto Rico. We begin this chapter with some questions about all pension funds. Why should you believe the promise of a pension fund that says it will send you a defined amount of money from the time of your retirement for the rest of your life? This promise may stretch 40 or 50 years or more into an unknown future. Whose promise is it exactly? Do you understand that a pension fund can go broke? If it does, should somebody else pay? Should your fellow taxpayers pay for your pension if your pension fund fails?

Defined benefit pension plans are a large factor in our financial system. As of the second quarter of 2021, the total assets of U.S. private and public defined benefit pension plans were $11 trillion, while their liabilities were estimated at $17 trillion, FSOC reported,[1] an enormous $6 trillion shortfall.

Some of the shortfalls faced by pension funds are due to the Federal Reserve's keeping long-term interest rates very low for a very long time, which affects all pension funds, just as it does individual savers. The historic super-low interest rate environment has made relatively safe investments, once deemed the most appropriate for pension funds, yield returns below the level the pension plans need to keep pace with their obligations. Sponsors of pension plans are left with two alternatives: either to increase

134

the amounts of the contributions they make to the plans, or to invest the plan assets in higher-risk or illiquid assets such as high-yield debt, private equity funds, hedge funds, or real estate. Sponsors often understandably prefer not to make or require bigger contributions; hence, more risk is taken. This feels good when riskier markets are rising and bad when they fall.

Pension funds can generally be categorized into private single-employer plans; multiemployer plans; and public pension plans. Private single-employer plans are on average in much better shape than the other two pension plan types.

The "funded ratio" is the ratio of a plan's assets to its estimated liabilities. The funded ratio of the 100 largest private, single-employer defined benefit plans was estimated to be 97 percent in September 2021, or a funding deficit of 3 percent, albeit following an unsustainable rate of asset appreciation during the post-pandemic stock market boom and Everything Bubble.

The long-term trend in pension plans is against the formation of new single-employer plans and in favor of the formation of individual 401(k) accounts, the investments of which are owned by each individual employee with no further promise from the employer. This trend reflects the fact that defined benefit plans are hard to manage and risky for the employer and may be risky for the beneficiaries, as well. When a company establishes a single-employer defined benefit plan, it effectively guarantees the pension plan, and the assets of the company are available to support the plan as a matter of law. Any funding deficit of the pension plan is a debt of the company. But companies can and do go bankrupt. Then for any funding deficit, the pension fund becomes an unsecured creditor, among all the other creditors, of the bankrupt estate. Notable very large examples were the bankruptcies of General Motors and Chrysler in 2009. About General Motors, once the top corporation in the world and a triple-A credit, it was later wittily said, "It used to be a company with a pension fund, it became a pension fund with a company."

Brooding on this fundamental risk in 1961, Nat Weinberg, a senior economist of the United Auto Workers union, invented the idea of getting the government to insure their pensions. If we are going to negotiate for bigger pensions, which the auto companies may not be able to pay, he cleverly reasoned, let's get the government to guarantee them. Weinberg's idea, brilliant as a political strategy for the UAW but generating great moral hazard for everybody concerned, resulted in the creation of the Pension Benefit Guaranty Corporation (PBGC) as an instrumentality of the federal government in 1974. The chartering statute claimed that the government was not on the hook for the PBGC's obligations and that the PBGC would be financially on its own—but of course this proved not to be true. It had an "implied" government guarantee, not a formal one, but such an implied guarantee always turns out to be real, as became unmistakably clear with the 2021 multiemployer pension bailout legislation.

The Bailout of Another "Implied" Government Guarantee

The PBGC provides a guarantee for pension plan beneficiaries. Theoretically, but not actually, independent of the U.S. Treasury, it has two financially separate programs: single-employer plans and multiemployer plans. Of these, the multiemployer insurance program was historically in much worse financial condition. For its 2020 fiscal year, the PBGC reported a combined net worth deficit of $48 billion, driven by the insolvent multiemployer program's $64 billion deficit. The actual looming deficit may have been much larger than what was presented by the PBGC's accounting conventions.

Then for its 2021 fiscal year, which included the effects of the Congressional bailout of multiemployer pension plans, the PBGC reported a surplus of $0.5 billion for its multiemployer program, slightly solvent instead of hopelessly insolvent. Saved by the bailout. The taxpayers lost, and the multiemployer pension plans and the PBGC won.

Multiemployer pension plans, like the PBGC itself, are a creation of organized labor. They are employee benefit plans maintained under one or more collective bargaining agreements to which more than one employer contributes. Often the plan sponsor is a board of trustees consisting of equal representation from the labor union and employers' management—a perfect recipe for a deal in which pension obligations are increased but not funded. Multiemployer plans are typically found in industries or parts of the country where a number of employers have collective bargaining agreements with a union whose members may perform tasks for more than one of the employers. For example, the Teamsters union maintains a multiemployer plan with a number of supermarket chains for truckers who make deliveries to those supermarkets. As of 2018, there were 2,472 multiemployer pension plans with 15.5 million participants and beneficiaries.[2] That is about 6 percent of the U.S. adult population. The PBGC's Fiscal Year 2020 Projections Report estimated the total unfunded pension liabilities of PBGC-insured multiemployer plans at $757 billion, based on 2018 data.[3] While the PBGC believed that most multiemployer plans were likely to remain solvent, it recognized that a large number appeared unable to avoid insolvency. Indeed, according to the PBGC 2019 projections, 124 multiemployer plans had declared that they would likely run out of money over the next 20 years.[4] Why were multiemployer plans in so much worse shape than single-employer plans? Why were they in need of being given money from the taxpayers in order to survive?

Some of the problems of multiemployer funds are historical. Many experienced significant asset growth in the 1990s and, rather than storing those surpluses for the inevitable rainy days, chose to increase benefits instead. When the surpluses dissipated in the succeeding decade, the increase in benefits became unaffordable. In addition, many of these plans exist in older industries that have declined, which leads to a downward spiral: the exit of numerous employers causes the remaining employers in the plans to bear increased funding burdens, and at the same time to decrease the work force so there are fewer workers to make contributions and a higher ratio of those receiving payments to those making payments. This demonstrates the dangers of mak-

ing such long-term promises into an unknown future and planning to fund them later.

Structural features inherent in the design of these plans create
chronic problems. Decisions to increase contributions or to cut
benefits are often not possible because of the even mix of employer
and labor representatives on plan boards. Employers have often
not made sufficient contributions to these plans partially because
figuring out the proper amount for each employer to contribute
involves estimating the financial health and future solvency of
the other employers in the plan. Fuzzy accounting requirements
have often obscured the real amount of underfunding. Employers
were not required to make the amount of contributions necessary
to fully fund the plans. All of these problems with multiemployer
plans were present long before the Covid pandemic.

The problems with multiemployer plans are exacerbated by
the PBGC's own finances. Before the 2021 bailout, the PBGC
projected that there was a high likelihood that its own multiemployer insurance program would itself become insolvent, in the
sense of flat out running out of money, by 2026 and that there was
a near certainty of such insolvency by the end of fiscal year 2027.[5]
It would then have no assets while still having huge liabilities. But
by 2020, it was already deeply insolvent in the sense of having liabilities greater than its assets.

In an essay written in 2019, Alex proposed that one of the key
causes of multiemployer plan deficits was the very existence of
the PBGC's guarantee program itself. The government guarantee
induces pension plans to make bigger pension commitments than
they can fund, because of the expectation that the government
will pay if the plans deteriorate.[6] Unfortunately for the U.S. taxpayer, this expectation proved to be exactly correct.

The PBGC states in its Annual Reports that, "ERISA [the fed-
eral law that established the PBGC] provides that the U.S. gov-
ernment is not liable for any obligation or liability incurred by the
PBGC." Nice idea, but it should have reminded you, Informed
Reader, of the "implied" federal guarantee of the obligations of
Fannie Mae and Freddie Mac. That turned out to be a real guar-

antee of $190 billion when Fannie and Freddie were bailed out after their 2008 failure. Now once again with multiemployer pensions, we have seen the normal coming home to roost of such risk turkeys, as the federal government provided a huge bailout of the multiemployer pension plans. The bailout was facilitated by the political environment of overall unrestrained government spending triggered by the Covid crisis, and the opportunity to use other people's money was successfully seized.

In the Butch Lewis Emergency Pension Plan Relief Act of 2021, a part of the American Rescue Plan Act, Congress provided a bailout that will pay insolvent or critically troubled multiemployer plans "such amount required for the plan to pay all benefits due during the period beginning on the date of payment of the special financial assistance payment under this section and ending on the last day of the plan year ending in 2051"! In interim regulations, the PBGC confirmed that the plans would be paid enough additional money to avoid insolvency until then. In other words, Congress elected to subsidize these plans for 30 years, at an estimated cost of $86 billion according to the Congressional Budget Office (CBO). This probably sets up multiemployer plans to need a further taxpayer bailout in 30 years, when the current legislators will be long out of office. This unhappy fact is brought out in shocking clarity by the PBGC's own estimate of a new most likely insolvency date for its multiemployer program: 2055, only four years after the bailout payments end.[7] So it is that the taxpayers, most of whom do not have a defined benefit pension themselves, are forced to pay for the insolvencies of the multiemployer plans and of the PBGC.

Whenever there is a taxpayer bailout, it always should be, and usually is, accompanied by reforms designed to ensure that the problems that caused the bailout do not recur. The Dodd-Frank Act of 2010 is a good example—there Congress was trying to fix the problems of the Housing Bubble. Likewise, the Financial Institutions Reform, Recovery, and Enforcement Act of 1989 was designed to fix the savings and loan problems of the 1980s. However, the multiemployer plan bailout contained in the American

Rescue Plan Act made *no structural reforms at all*, so the inherent weaknesses that plague multiemployer plans are guaranteed to continue.

An iron principle of bailouts should be: *No reform, no bailout*. But the 2021 act presents the opposite and very unwise approach of "Big bailout, no reform." The complete lack of reform, combined with the demonstration that, once again, the "implied" guarantee is fully real, and that the politicians will always stick the taxpayers with its costs, further increases the moral hazard of government pension guarantees going forward.

The $86 billion cost of this bailout is merely an estimate, not a limit. There is no cap on the cost contained in the legislation or anywhere else, and there is no telling how large this bailout could become if the troubled multiemployer plans continue in their past ways. Some analysts have suggested that the CBO estimate may be low, citing that just one troubled multiemployer pension plan, the Central States, Southeast & Southwest Areas Pension Plan, has by itself a reported funding shortfall of approximately $44 billion.[8] Another factor indicating that the CBO estimate may be low is that both multiemployer pension plans and public pension plans are allowed to measure their liabilities using their own estimated discount rates, which often assume investment returns higher than those actually achieved. Many economists believe this rule has led to consistent understatements of the actual amount of liabilities and thus to large understatements of the deficits of multiemployer pension plans.[9]

Multiemployer plans were supposed to be self-sustaining with the backup of the PBGC, which was also supposed to be self-sustaining. Obviously, both presumptions turned out to be false. These problems long preceded the pandemic and the 2020 panic and would have been critical had the pandemic never occurred, although the pandemic may have exacerbated them. To characterize the massive bailout of multiemployer funds in the American Rescue Plan Act as pandemic relief was disingenuous, to put it mildly. It was an excuse, not a reason.

The American mainstream press failed miserably to point out the lack of reform and promulgated the mischaracterization of the bailout as pandemic relief. That there has been no public demand for reform of the multiemployer system may reflect that the financial complexity of the structures makes the problems difficult to understand. And, of course, the recipients of the bailout money were able to take advantage of the disappearance of public resistance to astronomical government budget deficits.

Public Pensions

We now turn to an even more troubled pension fund sector: public pension funds, or the pension plans for the employees of states and municipalities. The United States has about 6,000 public pension plans with about $4.4 trillion in assets and more than 25 million current and retired participants,[10] or about 10 percent of the adult population. In June 2021, the aggregate funded status of the 100 largest U.S. public defined pension plans was only about 83 percent, even after being helped by asset price appreciation from the stock market boom and the one-time infusion of funds from the American Rescue Plan.

Considering only the pension plans sponsored by states, a September 2021 report by The Pew Charitable Trusts, written with an optimistic tone, estimates that state pension plans finished the 2021 fiscal year in their least bad condition since the 2007–09 financial crisis, and projected that state retirement plans were now 84 percent funded by the date of the report.[11] While 84 percent may sound pretty good, perhaps making you think of getting a grade of B, recall that 84 percent means that their assets are 16 percent smaller than their liabilities—or alternatively, that their liabilities are 19 percent greater than their assets. A bank in that situation would be closed down. Still, that is not as bad as the funded ratios of multiemployer and many other public pension plans.

Pew attributes the improvement in state pension plans to market returns of more than 25 percent in fiscal year 2021—the highest market returns in 30 years—and to substantial increases in the amount of contributions states made to their public pension plans. According to Pew, even the four most troubled pension systems, those of Illinois, Kentucky, Pennsylvania, and New Jersey, showed increased contributions to their plans over the past decade. Pew also finds that nearly every state has initiated pension reforms, including cutting pension benefits for new hires. As a result, Pew projects the aggregate unfunded pension liability for the states might be "only" $1 trillion.

We observe that markets will not produce a 25-percent return every year, as the Everything Bubble adjusts to reality. We are seeing this already in the market declines in early 2022. Pew recognizes that slower market growth could trigger the need for states to further increase pension fund contributions, which could be difficult for some states where pension fund contributions already consume 15 percent of state revenues. The ability of states to increase pension contributions in 2021 was enhanced by bailout funds provided by the American Rescue Plan Act and other federal pandemic-related subsidies. These funds will run out in time. In the states with the most underfunding, maintaining a high contribution level will be very difficult, in view of steadily increasing pension costs. Pew points out that employer pension costs in Illinois, Kentucky, New Jersey, and Pennsylvania collectively experienced a 300-percent increase between 2009 and 2019. This projected funding status relates only to pension plans actually run by the 50 states themselves and does not include the thousands of plans run by state subdivisions, the cities, counties, and other municipalities.

The real situation is likely to be worse because of the questionable accounting permitted for public pension plans (and for multiemployer plans, though not for single-employer private pension plans). Public pension fund sponsors, like multiemployer plans, are permitted to assume investment returns based on their own long-run expectations or hopes. As a result, public pension funds that do not meet their assumed return may be overstating their funded status, so the aggregate funding shortfall for these funds may be even more than the staggering amounts reported.[12] In the meantime, as noted above, the push for increased investment earnings has driven many public investment plans into relatively risky alternative investments.

By allocating $350 billion to state and local governments, the American Rescue Plan Act temporarily eased public pension fund woes, despite the Act's explicit blanket prohibition that "No State or territory may use funds made available under this section for deposit into any pension fund."[13] The Treasury Department subsequently interpreted this broad prohibition to cover only "a payment into a pension fund if both: (1) the payment reduces a liability incurred prior to the start of the COVID-19 public health emergency, and (2) the payment occurs outside the recipient's regular timing for making such payments."[14] The Treasury went on to state that Rescue Act funds may be used to make regularly scheduled current contributions to pension funds based on a predetermined percentage of employee wages and salaries.[15] Treasury's final regulations, adopted in January 2022, added a restriction that to be permissible a payment could not be larger than a regular payment would have been.[16] Since money is fungible, however, if Rescue Act funds are used for other purposes, thereby freeing up money to fund pension plans, it is hard to see how the Congressional prohibition would be effective in any event, even if it were interpreted more strictly than it has been by Treasury. But here is the main point: even if the entire $350 billion had been allocated to fund troubled public pension plans, it would be a drop in the bucket compared to the deficit they face.

Illinois Again

To show how bad a public pension plan problem can be, let us again consider the state with the worst public pension problems—Illinois. Illinois and the governmental entities in the state have 667 government-employee pension funds that cover more than a million government employees and retirees and feature a huge combined deficit. Illinois state pension plans were underfunded by $144 billion at June 30, 2020, according to the state's own reckoning. According to Moody's calculations, using more conservative discount rates[17] to calculate the present value of future benefits owed to retirees, the shortfall was $313 billion.[18] It's a little disorienting to be faced with these numbers in the hundreds of billions of dollars, isn't it, Faithful Reader?

This huge deficit, however measured, covers only the five employee pension funds actually run by the State of Illinois and does not cover the other 662 government employee pension plans in Illinois, particularly those of the City of Chicago, which are also deeply, perhaps hopelessly, underfunded. Other analysts have compiled estimates of the combined shortfalls of all these plans, based on requests to Moody's and the reports of individual pension plans, which suggest that Illinois' overall public pension deficit, calculated using Moody's methodology, was approximately $530 billion. The Illinois government estimates $303 billion for the total deficit.[19] According to Pew Charitable Trusts, Illinois' state pension plans are only 39 percent funded, which is the lowest funded rate in the nation.[20] Stated alternately, they have a 61-percent funding deficit. Payments to the state's pension plans consume a quarter of the State of Illinois' budget. Illinois has the lowest credit rating from Standard & Poor's, Moody's Investor Service, and Fitch Ratings of any state, despite recent upgrades.[21]

How did Illinois get itself into this mess?

Illinois' state pension plans are defined benefit pension plans, so government employees receive pension payments for life determined by a formula. As with all standard defined benefit plans, the formula has no relationship to whether the pension fund has the money to pay them or not. The right to these payments as defined by the formula, even if the formula has results no one expected, is protected absolutely by the Illinois Constitution, Article XIII, Section 5. This describes pension membership as "an enforceable contractual relationship" that "shall not be diminished or impaired."

The Illinois Supreme Court has interpreted this language strictly, using it to strike down all efforts to reform the pension plans or modify pension benefits to make them affordable to the Illinois taxpayers.[22] Of course, individual taxpayers can react by leaving Illinois, which had the second-highest population loss among all states in the decade 2010–2020.

The level of benefits and the extent of the contributions for public pension plans are typically determined by negotiations between the relevant governmental entity and labor unions representing the public employees. The politicians who run the governmental entities are often dependent on the labor unions for political endorsements and political contributions. It is not required that the pension contributions be sufficient to fund the benefits promised, so the shortfall can be and has been accumulated as off-balance-sheet debt.

Moreover, Illinois state and local pension plans set only a 90-percent funding goal, which means by definition that they target a deficit. Assets would be 10 percent smaller than liabilities, even if the goal were achieved. A 100-percent funding goal is what is financially sound.

That this model has failed in Illinois is obvious. The Illinois pension funds would be broke with or without the Covid pandemic, with or without the 2020 financial panic, and with or without the post-crisis asset price boom. However, the Covid financial crisis did add one special mention for Illinois, as it became the only state in history ever to borrow from the Federal Reserve. The founders of the Federal Reserve would surely have staggered with disbelief had they been told their creation would one day lend money to an insolvent state government.

The aggregate shortfalls for The City of Chicago's pension plans, including its four city pension funds, the Chicago Teacher's Pension Fund, and the Park District Pension Fund, have an aggregate shortfall of $50 billion, a Wirepoints analysis for fiscal year 2020 calculates, using government-supplied numbers. But based on Moody's calculations, it was $97 billion. Looking at Cook County, which includes Chicago, for its three county pension funds, the government-supplied deficit is $9 billion and the Moody's estimate is $25 billion. For a variety of suburban and downstate pension funds for which Moody's does not supply data, the government-supplied deficit was $32 billion.[23] Based on the most recent data they had access to in July 2021, Standard and Poor's reports that of the 250 Illinois public safety (police and fire) pension plans they have data for, the average funded ratio was only 52 percent.[24]

According to the Illinois Policy Institute, most Illinois government employees contribute only about 4 to 8 percent (8 to 16 percent if interest earned on investments is included) of what they will receive in retirement. For example, for the State Universities Retirement System members who retired between 2013 and 2015, the employee on average contributed about $145,000, but will get $2.2 million in lifetime payments under the plan's formula with 30 years of service.[25]

Consider that 30 years of service and pension eligibility could be reached when the employees are in their early or mid-50s. The Illinois Policy Institute reports that 60 percent of state workers retire in their 50s, many with full retirement benefits.

In Chicago, based on information derived from a 2013 study, nearly half of all city workers retired before age 60. They had an average pension, for those with 30 or more years of service, of $65,000. Although this study is several years old, it displays the key structural problem of making pensions more expensive by starting to pay them long before normal retirement age.

S&P Global Ratings blames the following for the weakness of Illinois municipal pension funds: "poor funding discipline in the past, inability to reform benefits, weak statutory funding requirements, weak demographic trends, and limited revenue-raising flexibility or political unwillingness to raise revenue."[26] They need to add as a cause the moral hazard created by the Illinois Constitution.

Forbes Magazine blamed Illinois' pension crisis on inordinately high public employee salaries, including tree trimmers in Chicago making $106,663, nurses at state corrections institutions making $277,100 and junior college presidents making $491,095. It estimated that with about 13 million residents in Illinois, each one owes $19,000 on an estimated $251 billion unfunded pension liability.[27] As discussed, others estimate the unfunded pension liability much higher. Using Wirepoints' 2020 estimate of a total statewide pension funding deficit of $530 billion, each individual in Illinois is on the hook for $40,000 and each Illinois household for $110,000.

Is there a solution for these massively insolvent pension plans of Illinois? Can Illinois tax its way out of the predicament? As we write, it has among the highest sales tax and property tax rates in the country and has a flat income tax rate of 4.95 percent. In 2020, Illinois Governor J.B. Pritzker tried to increase state tax revenues through a progressive income tax referendum, but this failed at the polls. There is always the problem that heavy tax increases to pay for past deficits may drive away residents and businesses and further weaken the state's economy and finances.

A structural reform that naturally comes to mind is a constitutional amendment allowing for pension reforms, including changes in pension formulas, reductions in pensions for those not yet retired, or later retirement ages. We anticipate there will be no political will for that, as so far there has not been. Of course, the state *should* amend its Constitution to reform the pension plan provisions, but it won't.

The fact is that decades of promising payments without providing the money to pay for them, the interlock between government employee unions and politicians, optimistic hopes of investment returns, and the Illinois Constitution, have placed Illinois in a position equivalent to having run up all of one's credit cards to the limit.

Unlike a credit card borrower, states under the U.S. Constitution cannot declare bankruptcy to reorganize their debts. As discussed in Chapter 9, they could in theory default, as nine states, including Illinois, did in the 1840s, when a federal bailout by assumption of the state debt was proposed but rejected.

The strategy Illinois must now prefer is to try to stave off disaster, and as we write, with the Democratic Party in control of both the Presidency and Congress, as well as the Illinois government, to work for a federal taxpayer bailout. But will the citizens of North Dakota and Texas be happy to pay for Chicago's unaffordable pensions? The American Recovery Plan's bailout of multiemployer pension plans, its grants to states, and the Federal Reserve's making loans to Illinois, suggest that an Illinois bailout may be possible—depending, of course, on the results of future elections.

Using Moody's calculations, Illinois combines the worst funded ratio with the biggest pension deficits of any state, but other states have serious pensions trouble, too.

Table 10.1 lists the ten states with the largest pension deficits, as estimated by Moody's, for the 2021 fiscal year, beginning with the worst. It adds the corresponding funded ratios, based on state-provided numbers, calculated by Pew Charitable Trusts for the 2019 fiscal year, as the most recent data available. The table only considers state-run pension plans. If all the local plans were added in, the numbers would be far worse.

With multiple states in deep pension deficit debt, we imagine that if one gets a federal bailout, so will others. It looks to us like a pension bailout with federal taxpayer funds could potentially become the largest bailout in history. This would be a bailout cre-

TABLE 10.1
State Pension Funding Data

	Pension Deficit (Moody's 2021) in billions	Funded Ratio (Pew 2019)
Illinois	$312.6	38.9%
California	$240.4	71.9%
Texas	$172.8	69.0%
New Jersey	$151.7	39.7%
Massachusetts	$109.7	59.4%
Pennsylvania	$95.6	58.0%
Connecticut	$90.1	44.4%
Maryland	$69.4	71.6%
Kentucky	$56.3	44.6%
Michigan	$51.7	61.1%

ated by giving the alliance between state and local politicians and public employee labor unions the power to use pension funds to evade limitations on state debt, and to run up the resulting off-balance sheet debt to unpayable amounts.

CHAPTER 11

Student Loans

A Failed Government Lending Program

STUDENT LOANS have become a truly big market, with $1.8 trillion in outstanding debt in 2021, of which $1.6 trillion are federal student loans, which means that they are guaranteed by the federal government. As shown in Graph 11.1, this debt doubled in the last ten years and has grown to more than 3½ times as large as it was in 2006.

GRAPH 11.1

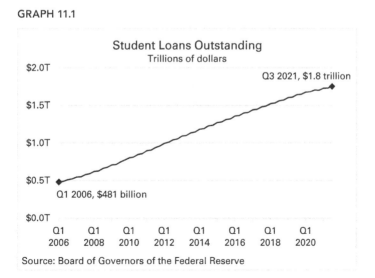

Student Loans Outstanding
Trillions of dollars

Q3 2021, $1.8 trillion

Q1 2006, $481 billion

Source: Board of Governors of the Federal Reserve

The expansion of student debt, granted mostly without credit underwriting and with the loan proceeds turning immediately into college revenues, is both a cause of and is deeply intertwined with the unaffordable escalation of the costs of college over the past several decades. It is likewise intertwined with politics and a vivid case of how easy government credit with no credit underwriting helps drive up the price of what is being financed.

In his 2021 book, *The Debt Trap,* Josh Mitchell rightly says:

> Student debt enabled schools to raise tuition faster than family incomes, creating a higher-education industrial complex that has driven up the price of college and graduate school to unprecedented levels. . . . Student debt is both a cause and consequence of those higher costs. . . . This is the never-ending chase of college pricing: The more colleges raise tuition, the more Americans borrow. The more Americans borrow, the more colleges raise tuition.

The financial result of this, Mitchell writes, is that "Of the $1.6 trillion in student debt, borrowers are on track to pay back only two-thirds, leaving taxpayers on the hook for more than $500 billion"—which is certainly consistent with the subtitle of his book, "How Student Loans Became a National Catastrophe."[1]

The great expansion of student loans dates back to the Higher Education Act of 1965. Upon signing this act, President Lyndon Johnson said, "The path of knowledge is open to all who have the determination to walk it." At the same time, the door to government money was opened to the colleges, which did not and do not suffer any losses when the loans default. A college president of the time shrewdly observed, "We are quite suddenly confronted by a munificence on the part of the federal government."[2]

Of course, the designers of the 1965 Act could not have imagined how their creation would evolve and grow, how big its losses would become, or how those losses would be escalated by the Covid crisis. An interesting insight into the political origin of the student loan program is provided in Paul Volcker's autobiography,

Keeping At It. Volcker recounts that when he was a deputy under-secretary in the Treasury Department in the 1960s:

> I was asked during the Johnson administration to lead an interagency study to propose how the federal government might encourage access to low-cost student loans. It was a hot issue and a number of approaches were being tested by state and local governments and private entities. We proposed waiting to "let a thousand flowers bloom" and determine later what justified intervention from the federal government. I remember the response from the White House assistant assigned to oversee our study: "Forget about this. There is an election ahead. We're going to have a program, it's going to be a federal program, and President Johnson is going to get credit for it."[3]

And so it was.

Today, in the wake of the Covid crisis, we are forced to recognize the utter failure of this student loan program as a loan program. To be a success, any loan program has to generate at least enough income to cover the losses on the loans it makes that don't pay. Federal student loans fall miles short of this minimal standard. The loss to the taxpayers on this program would have been a big number in any case, since nonpayment rates were very high even before the Covid crisis, but when the effects of the pandemic and the political responses to it are added, the loss gets still bigger. If a generalized student loan forgiveness, often proposed by various politicians, were implemented, it would make the loss enormous.

Some politicians and borrowers clearly like the idea of loans that do not have to be repaid, making them effectively a welfare program or a grant by another name, but federal student loans were sold and enacted as a loan program, and as a loan program they're a flop.

In 2010, President Barack Obama claimed about nationalizing student loans, "This reform will save taxpayers $68 billion."

The profits on government student loans were then supposed to pay for part of the cost of Obamacare and help reduce the federal deficit.[4]

The outcome was different. As reported in June 2021, the Biden administration estimated that "Total losses from the federal government's student debt portfolio will cost taxpayers $68 billion."[5]

This is quite a striking pair of numbers: from *plus* $68 billion to *minus* $68 billion. But the actual losses are much greater than that.

One political response to the Covid pandemic was to defer any payments and stop accrual of interest on federal student loans—a "pause" in repayment, which kept being extended, to May 2022 as we write, by executive actions. This resulted in spending government and taxpayer money without Congressional appropriations because interest owed the government is in effect given to the borrowers. That is helpful to the borrowers' budgets, but needless to say, expensive to the government's budget. It alone will reportedly cost more than the previously estimated total loss of $68 billion:

"The pause in student-debt repayment has cost the federal government more than $100 billion since the start of the pandemic," The *Wall Street Journal* wrote in January 2022, "and could cost $4 billion to $5 billion a month until the moratorium is lifted . . . according to government estimates."[6]

The Department of Education happily announced that it will save borrowers $5 billion per month. Someone else will have to speak for the taxpayers who will have to pick up the $5 billion a month tab. (While perusing these billions, it is interesting to reflect that when the government's losses on student loans reached $239 *million* in 1974, it was considered a big issue.)

How many billions, or hundreds of billions, of dollars are the student loan losses going to cost the taxpayers in the end? We have seen that Mitchell cited a staggering loss of $500 billion. This estimate came from a study commissioned in 2018 by the Secretary of Education and performed by a former senior officer of JPMorgan, Jeff Courtney. His calculations, including that the government will ultimately recover between 51 and 63 cents on the dollar of defaulted student loans, led to the $500 billion loss estimate.[7]

Among the first acts of the Biden administration's Education Department, in February 2021, was to end any use of this study.

An alternative reaction might have been to get a market test of Courtney's estimates and of the value of their student loans by putting a pool of them up for sale, with no government guarantee or support, and see what anyone would bid for them. What price do you suppose you would bid, Thoughtful Reader?

In the meantime, senior political voices of the Democratic Party argued for forgiveness of unpaid government student loans, perhaps of up to $50,000 per borrower. A Brookings Institution article estimated that this would cost the taxpayers $1 trillion. Forgiveness up to $10,000 per borrower has also been suggested— the same Brookings article says this would cost $373 billion.[8]

On top of those mind-boggling numbers, the idea of broad-based forgiveness of defaulted and otherwise unpaid loans raises a fundamental fairness question: How about the borrowers who diligently paid their loans off? What do they get in return for their responsible behavior, and why not treat them equally by having the government refund what they paid?

A second question is that if you create the precedent of a generalized forgiveness, how can you expect future borrowers to take their debt seriously as something they need to repay? In fact, to propose such forgiveness is to confirm the failure of student loans as a loan program.

Student Loans, Subprime Mortgages, and Skin in the Game

The Student Loan Catastrophe, a 2017 book by Richard Fossey, maintained that "higher education is sustained by a student loan bubble." We think a more precise statement would be that *the bloated price of higher education* is sustained by the student loan bubble. Fossey continued, "There are eerie similarities [to] the housing market before it crashed."⁹ We agree. The inflated prices of houses were sustained by the subprime mortgage lending bubble, and in both cases, loans were made without considering how or whether they could be repaid.

There are other provocative parallels between student loans and the low credit quality mortgages that inflated the infamous housing bubble of the early 2000s. In both cases, the government energetically promoted plausible goals—higher education and home ownership—to excess, choosing the unwise method of overexpansion of debt—expansion to levels unrepayable for a large percentage of the borrowers. In both cases, the government guaranteed the credit—virtually all of it in student loans and much of it in mortgages. In both cases, the government put the risk of bad loans on those who pay taxes. In both cases, the debt expansion drove up the price of the thing being financed, colleges and houses, to heights sustainable only if the debt could always be increasing. In both cases, the risk came home to roost.

We can very usefully apply one of the most fundamental lessons from the disastrous mortgage bubble to student loans. This is: the need for "skin in the game." Skin in the game means that those who originate the credit and make money from it must keep for their own account some of the risk, so that they share in the loss if things go badly.

After the housing crisis, it was nearly universally agreed upon that those who create risk in mortgage finance should retain a part of that risk, and that the "originate and sell" model was an important part of the problem. "Originate and sell" was memorably demonstrated by many subprime mortgage brokers who promoted and originated risky loans with a high propensity to default, made money on their sale, and got somebody else to take and later pay for the risk. That "somebody else" eventually included the taxpayers, through the bailouts of Fannie Mae and Freddie Mac and others. In contrast, skin in the game aligns the incentives of the originators of the loans with the taxpayer guarantors to control excesses in riskiness and debt expansion. For mortgages, a version of skin in the game was adopted by the

Dodd-Frank Act of 2010, but a better version had already been developed by the Federal Home Loan Banks.

The Mortgage Partnership Finance (MPF) program (of which Alex led the development) was created by the Federal Home Loan Banks and instructively displayed the advantages of skin in the game.[10] In Original MPF, which was introduced in 1997, the originator holds a continuing credit risk for the life of all the mortgage loans placed in the program, is paid for doing so, and bears credit losses if they exceed the expected low level. The result of this alignment of interests, unsurprisingly, was high credit quality performance, which continued through the housing finance crisis of 2007–09.

Applying the mortgage experience to student loans, we see that for a great many students, colleges play a role similar to a subprime mortgage broker: promoting risky loans with a high propensity to default, in this case taking all the cash from the proceeds of the loans as revenue, spending it, and passing on all the credit risk to somebody else—namely, to the U.S. Treasury and thence to the taxpayers.

So, the most important parties who need to have skin in the student loan game are the colleges. They are the effective subprime loan brokers, the originators, and the promoters, who promote the loans without regard to how they will be repaid or what the risks of their nonpayment are. Since the loans become revenue to them, they are the chief financial beneficiaries of student loans— the recipients of the "munificence of the federal government," as the college president said decades ago. It is their escalating costs that are fed by the loans, resulting in ever more debt and more risk of nonpayment. As the former chief of staff for a member of Congress who worked for years on student loan issues wrote, "Higher [student] loan limits lead to higher tuition and fees. Schools waste the money in numerous ways, including armies of administrators, lower teaching loads, higher salaries and fancy buildings."[11]

It is indeed a sweet deal to create the risk, keep all the money, and stick the taxpayers with the losses.

We believe the incentives of the student loan program need fundamental realignment. The federal student loan program should require that all colleges that receive the proceeds of student loans should have skin in the game in the form of financial responsibility for a serious share of the losses generated by nonpayment of the loans. It does not have to be all the losses, just a material share—we think 20 percent would do the job. The colleges would thus stand to take losses on bad loans along with the taxpayers, as they should, as pari passu risk-takers in a 20–80 ratio. As a matter of equity, as Nassim Nicholas Taleb wrote in his book, *Skin in the Game*, "If you inflict risk on others, and they are harmed, you need to pay some price for it."[12]

A general principle of finance is that debt pushed by those who have no skin in the game and no stake in the credit performance is likely to have high defaults. Even if all the tens or hundreds of billions in losses of the current federal student loan program were somehow paid for by a fairy godmother and the program allowed to start over from scratch, the deep incentive conflict at its very core would continue.

It follows that disastrous student loan outcomes will continue as long as colleges have no skin in the student loan game, and they need to be given some.

In 2019, Senator Lamar Alexander proposed a skin in the game idea, describing it as "a new accountability system [for colleges] based upon whether borrowers are actually repaying their student loans." Unfortunately, this sound proposal was not enacted. The annual presidential budget document the same year correctly observed, "A better system would require postsecondary institutions that accept taxpayer funds to share in the financial responsibility associated with student loans."[13] So the concept is well understood, but of course most colleges do not want to be financially responsible for their own risk-creating actions. How surprising! It is certainly hard to stop big subsidies once the recipients get used to them and become a vocal constituency for the program.

At the end of his book on the student loan catastrophe, as he terms it, Josh Mitchell comes to the same conclusion that we have.[14] He writes:

> The student loan crisis is about perverse incentives. . . . A real fix would change those incentives, particularly for schools. It's no coincidence that when universities such as Stanford University and the University of Minnesota made loans to students directly—in the first half of the 20th century, before the government got into the loan business— default rates were low. When schools—or banks—put their own money at risk, they are more careful with it, and less likely to extend loans that will be impossible for borrowers to pay off. If student loans continue to be one of the primary ways the U.S. finances higher education, schools should put more of their own money at risk and suffer some losses if borrowers default.[15]

Mitchell points out that this would be consistent with "Lyndon Johnson's original vision . . . to have schools and the government contribute to an insurance fund that would guarantee student loans made by banks. If the borrower failed to repay, both schools and the government would suffer the losses."[16] We have wandered a long way from that concept. Of course, such insurance funds, as the discussion of the insolvency of the Pension Benefit Guarantee Corporation's multiemployer program in Chapter 10 makes obvious, can themselves go broke. Still, that original idea was a less flawed approach than what we've got now.

At present, we know of one private college which itself credit-enhances loans to its students under a fully private loan program, and has done so for years, with good credit results. This college wisely makes sure that the student borrowers understand that the money they are getting from the loan is debt that they must plan to pay back. Here is a good example of skin in the game working in student loans.

If federal student loans could progress to giving colleges some skin in the game, the colleges should have maximum flexibility for determining how they adapt to the new discipline. They could increase efficiency, reduce their costs and their prices, or at least control the inflation of their prices. They might shorten the time to graduation to scale back the need for borrowing. They should ensure that the students understand what loans mean and that they are expected to repay, consider their ability to repay, guide students to think about how the debt relates to their future prospects for income, adjust the mix of their programs, and come up with new ideas, just as happens in any competitive market, while managing the trade-offs involved. They should no longer play the role of subprime loan brokers.

Professor Richard Vedder, an expert in the causes of college cost inflation, trenchant critic of the foibles of higher education, and the author of *Going Broke by Degree*, wrote in December 2019:

> Make colleges become at least limited co-signers on loans—require them to have some skin in the game. Perhaps make the school liable for the first $5,000 of a defaulted loan, plus 20 percent of the balance over $5,000.
>
> Possibly excepting the 'skin in the game' idea, there is little short-term prospect for any improvement in our dysfunctional federal program for financially assisting college students.[17]

Rich, a good friend, also told Alex, "You should have 'skin in the game' put on your tombstone." (One could do worse.)

In the meantime, although it was clear enough before, the Covid crisis has removed any doubt that government student loans do not work as a loan program and as currently structured have demonstrated themselves to be a massive loss-making activity. To turn them off now would collapse the current finances of higher education and will not happen. As we try to look forward from early 2022, the saga is far from over.

CHAPTER 12

Central Banking to the Max

WE MET WALTER BAGEHOT and his famous and now well-practiced theory of how central banks should address financial crises in Chapter 3. Bagehot (1826–1877) published his great book on the nature of banking, *Lombard Street*, in 1873. His name has since become synonymous with the theory, energetically used and proved effective again in 2020, that in a financial crisis, the central bank should lend freely upon good collateral to the panicked market. This will calm the rush of having to sell assets at ever-falling prices to repay debt, and thus bridge the crisis to the return of more normal financial functioning. In verse, with apologies to Shakespeare:

> Tell me, where's the panic bred,
> In the world or in your head?
> How begot, how nourishèd?
> It's in your mind and eye.

> But when the Fed so great and fair
> Starts printing by the trillions there,
> You're sure Big Brother's taking care,
> And you go out and buy!

Bagehot's proposal was specifically meant for the Bank of England, the top bank in the world of his day, when the British pound sterling was the dominant international currency. His advice is now taken by all central banks, including the Bank of England, the European Central Bank, the Bank of Japan, and most importantly, by the current top central bank in the world, the Federal Reserve. As the issuer of the now-dominant international currency, the U.S. dollar, the Federal Reserve is in fact the central bank to the world.

Bagehot wrote: "Theory suggests, and experience proves, that in a panic the holders of the ultimate Bank reserve"—that is, what we now call the central bank—"should lend to all that bring good securities quickly, freely, and readily. By that policy they allay a panic; by every other policy they intensify it."[1]

Note that Bagehot proposed such crisis lending to "*all* that bring good securities," not just banks. "In most panics," he explained, "the principal use of a 'banking reserve' is not to advance to bankers; the largest amount is almost always advanced to the mercantile public and to bill-brokers."[2] The central bank must "lend to merchants, to minor bankers, to 'this man and that man,' whenever the security is good." A key insight is that Bagehot saw the central bank's "lender of last resort" function as lender to the financial system in general—just as it was in the spring of 2020.

In a crisis, there is another problem: "The evil is, that owing to the terror, what is commonly good security has ceased to be so." The definition of what is "good" collateral may need to be flexible.

Bagehot looked back from 1873 to the financial crisis England suffered in 1825, "a panic so tremendous that its results are well remembered after nearly fifty years"[3] (though perhaps not after nearly 200 years—eh, Reader?) That crisis featured defaults on Latin American debt, runs on banks, numerous bank failures, and a general dash for cash. What to do? Bagehot quoted Sir Robert Peel, later Prime Minister, who was Home Secretary at the time:

> "The intervention of the Bank [of England] was in any event absolutely necessary, and as its intervention would be chiefly useful by the effect which it would have in increasing the circulating medium, we advised the Bank to take the whole affair into their own hands at once. . . . They reluctantly consented."

Having consented to the government's wishes, "The success of the Bank of England upon this occasion was owing to its complete adoption of right principles," Bagehot maintained. In 1825,

> According to their official statement . . . the Bank directors "lent money by every possible means, and in modes which we had never adopted before; we took in stock on security, we purchased Exchequer Bills, we made advances on Exchequer Bills, we not only discounted outright, but we made advances on bills of Exchange to an immense amount—in short, by every possible means consistent with the safety of the Bank."[4]

Central bank lending "by every possible means, in modes never before adopted, to an immense amount"—in this respect, the 2020 Federal Reserve sounds a lot like the 1825 Bank of England. Of course, the amounts involved in financing the Covid panic would have been inconceivable to the bankers of 1825: instead of millions of pounds, there were trillions of dollars. But the fundamental principles were the same.

However, Bagehot was not satisfied by the Bank of England's past actions. He wanted the central bank to commit to *always* riding to the rescue of panicked financial markets. "The public have a right to know," he argued, "whether the Bank of England—the holders of our ultimate bank reserve—acknowledge this duty, and are ready to perform it. But this is now very uncertain." Further, "The public is never sure what policy will be adopted at the most important moment . . . until we have on this point a clear understanding with the Bank of England, both our liability to crises and our terror at crises will always be greater than they would otherwise be."[5]

Should the central bank make such a promise to always quell panics or should it keep its options open, with its responses kept uncertain in order to make financial actors appreciate that imprudence brings the risk of insolvency and failure? The objection to Bagehot's position, which was clearly argued at the time and since, is that by assuring financial actors that they will be bailed out by the central bank, you encourage speculation and excess debt. By protecting people against the risks of their behavior, you run up the risk, and thereby bring on the very crisis you wished to avoid.

Here is a perpetual issue in the theory of financial systems.

A former Governor of the Bank of England, Thomson Hankey, had argued at the time that Bagehot "has put forth what in my opinion is the most mischievous doctrine ever broached in the monetary or banking world." As *The Times* agreed, "It tends to aggravate panics, since it encourages other banks to push their trade to the utmost."[6]

We know, however, that financial markets may, without any explicit promise, decide that central bank bailouts are de facto a commitment, a promise reliably implied by the central bank's behavior and political imperatives. Thus, in the U.S., financial actors have believed in and experienced the "Greenspan Put,"[7] the "Bernanke Put," the "Yellen Put," and a continuing "Powell Put," named for the heads of the Federal Reserve during the last three decades. This is the belief that the Federal Reserve will always manipulate interest rates and print up the money so that monetary policy saves the day for the speculators. Recall from Chapter 2 how the Federal Reserve bailed out hedge fund speculators from their highly leveraged trades in U.S. Treasury securities at the height of the Covid panic. Have these "puts" of risk to the Federal Reserve themselves over time induced higher leverage and inflated asset prices, making the whole system more prone to failure? We cannot know that for sure, but it does seem likely and a point in favor of Thomson Hankey.

On the other hand, should the Federal Reserve and other central banks ever, even once, have stood aside in Olympian grandeur and let financial systems utterly crash, even if they deserved to? Surely not. That is the key argument in favor of Bagehot, and Bagehot has clearly won the historical debate, especially in the minds of the central bankers themselves, as so forcefully demonstrated again in 2020, when they applied Bagehot's theory to the max.

It worked to end the panic and restore financial market functioning. Then came, as it always does, the inevitable question: What do you do when the crisis is over?

This is an abiding problem. How can you reverse central bank and government emergency programs, originally thought to be and meant to be temporary, after the crisis has passed? The principle that such central bank and government interventions, required to survive in times of crisis, should be withdrawn in the renewed normal times which follow is the Cincinnatian Doctrine (discussed at length in Alex's *Finance and Philosophy*, Chapter 16).

The name comes from the ancient Roman hero, Cincinnatus, who was called from his plow to save the State, made temporary Dictator, did save the State, and then, mission accomplished, left his dictatorship and went back to his farm. Similarly, two millennia later, George Washington, a victorious general and hero who saved the new United States, voluntarily resigned his commission and went back to his farm.

But emergency interventions, however sincere the original intent that they would be temporary, inevitably build up economic and political constituencies who profit from them and want them to be continued indefinitely. For central bank monetization of government debt, the biggest such constituent is the government itself. Consider that the Federal Reserve's original "Quantitative Easing" or "QE" experiment, begun in 2009, was defended by Federal Reserve Chairman Ben Bernanke as a temporary program that in due course would be unwound. About QE, Bernanke testified to Congress in early 2011:

> Monetization would involve a permanent increase in the money supply to basically pay the government's bills through money creation. What we are doing here is a *temporary measure which will be reversed* so that at the end of the process, the money supply will be normalized, the amount of the Fed's balance sheet will be normalized, and there will be no permanent increase, either in the money outstanding, in the Fed's balance sheet, or in inflation.[8]

But QE is still with us eleven years later (as we write), the Federal Reserve balance sheet is more than three times as large as at the time of Bernanke's testimony, and the most rampant inflation since the 1980s is a daily feature in newspaper headlines and in the minds and pocketbooks of consumers.

The difficulty of winding emergency programs back down, once they have become established and profitable to their constituencies, is the Cincinnatian Problem. There is no easy answer to this problem. How, so to speak, do you get the Federal Reserve to go back to its farm when it has become the dominant bond and mortgage investor in the world?

In this context, we point out that central bank monetary actions pervade society and transfer wealth among various groups of people, which is an inherently political action. Monetary policies can cause consumer price inflations and also asset price inflations, like those in equities, houses, bonds, and cryptocurrencies that we are experiencing as we write. They can feed bubbles and consequent busts. They can calm a panic and finance a crisis. They can create negative real interest rates, or even negative nominal interest rates, and push investors into speculation. They can take money away from conservative savers and give it to leveraged speculators. They can transfer wealth from the people to the government without legislation, by creating an inflation tax. Central banks have become potent institutions, worthy of skeptical analysis. How long should their crisis actions be continued after the crisis?

The International Central Bank Asset Expansion

In 2020, as good students of Bagehot, and consistent with the Cincinnatian Doctrine, the Federal Reserve and other central banks printed however much money it took to finance the emergency responses to the Covid financial panic and economic contraction and to cover the related giant deficits of their governments. On the latter point, they carried out the unspoken first mandate of central banks: to finance the governments of which they are a part. As the Office of Financial Research wrote in its

2021 Annual Report, "For developed economies, particularly the
United States, Japan, and the larger European nations, central
banks purchased over 50% of new sovereign debt issuances."[9]

However, in contradiction to the Cincinnatian Doctrine, the
Federal Reserve did not stop monetizing bonds[10] and mortgages
in 2021 when economic growth had resumed, financial markets
were booming, house prices inflating in a new bubble, and consumer price inflation was rampant. It remained throughout 2021
the dominant buyer in the market and the Big Bid for Treasury
debt and for mortgage securities, creating the money to pay for
its continuing purchases and suppressing long-term interest rates.

We have already discussed in Chapter 3 the vast expansion of
the Federal Reserve balance sheet. By January 2022, it was up to
$8.9 trillion, which would have boggled the minds of the founders
of the Federal Reserve and all historical central bankers. It should
boggle your mind, too, Thoughtful Reader. Will this be "a temporary measure which will be reversed"?

The Federal Reserve in early 2022, as we write, has begun
discussing the possibility of shrinking its balance sheet. Federal
Reserve Chairman Jerome Powell "has said that it could take
another two or three meetings to firm up such plans, suggesting
that the process is likely to start no sooner than the middle of the
year [2022]."[11] We will see what happens.

In the meantime, the historic hyper-expansion of the Federal
Reserve's assets is so important that we look at it again. Its assets
doubled in 2009 to address the crisis of the time, doubled again
from then to 2014, and doubled again in 2020–21, as shown in
Graph 12.1.

Looking forward, if the Federal Reserve implements a Central
Bank Digital Currency, as discussed in Chapter 6, the additional
deposits created on its books with their corresponding assets will
have the effect of further ballooning its balance sheet.

The major central banks form a tight, international, elite club,
in close communication with each other, and tend to share the
same ideas. In our view, in a situation featuring great uncertainty
combined with great responsibility and intense communication

GRAPH 12.1

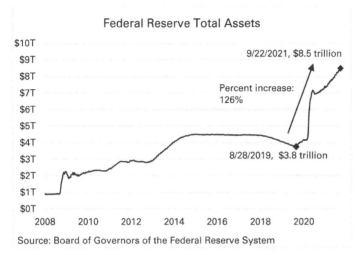

Federal Reserve Total Assets

Source: Board of Governors of the Federal Reserve System

among peers, cognitive herding is to be expected. To paraphrase a witty line of John Maynard Keynes, "A prudent banker is one who goes broke when everybody else goes broke." Similarly, perhaps a prudent central banker is one who prints money when everybody else is printing money.

Graph 12.2 shows the total assets of the European Central Banking System. They rapidly rose as the European sovereign debt crisis got central bank financing, accompanied by ECB President Mario Draghi's famous 2012 promise to do "Whatever it takes." After decreasing, the total assets rebounded again in 2015–17, in the times of the "Brexit" crisis, when Great Britain was leaving the European Union. Starting in 2020, their ascent became nearly vertical, reaching $9.7 trillion in September, or over $1 trillion more than the assets of the Federal Reserve. As shown in Table 12.8, the central bank assets per capita of population are nearly the same for the U.S. and the European Union.

Japan is the country with the world's third largest economy— or, if you consider the European Union one entity, the fourth. The total assets of its central bank, the Bank of Japan, are $6.6 trillion, as shown in Graph 12.3. The Bank of Japan has been a champion of Quantitative Easing, with central bank total assets

GRAPH 12.2

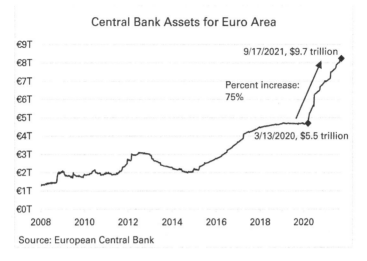

Central Bank Assets for Euro Area

Source: European Central Bank

per capita of population of more than twice the level of the U.S. or the European Union.

We turn to three smaller, but important central banks.

First, the Bank of England, the historically quintessential central bank, a leading model for the 20th-century international

GRAPH 12.3

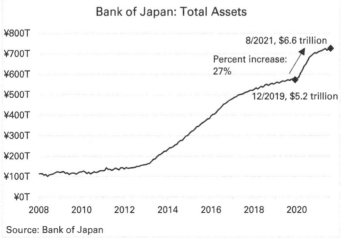

Bank of Japan: Total Assets

Source: Bank of Japan

spread of central banks, "The Old Lady of Threadneedle Street," the prime object of Walter Bagehot's arguments about what to do in a panic. Bagehot's heart would presumably have been warmed by the dramatic increase in the Bank of England's total assets in 2020 in response to the Covid crisis, as shown in Graph 12.4. But we suspect even he would have been very surprised that from 2008 to 2021, those assets multiplied more than ten times, as Graph 12.4 and also Table 12.7 show.

Switzerland is a small but rich country that financially punches above its weight. Its central bank, the Swiss National Bank, has among its assets a large portfolio of publicly traded U.S. stocks. Shares of its own stock trade on the Swiss stock exchange. Its total assets increased 20 percent in 2020–21—less than the others we are reviewing, but still significantly, as shown in Graph 12.5. As Table 12.8 shows, the Swiss National Bank is the all-time champion in central bank assets per capita of population, at over $119,000— more than five times the U.S. level. It is an interesting case of how large relative to its country a central bank might become.

Canada, like the U.S., spans the North American continent, but with a population and economy about one-tenth the size. As shown in Graph 12.6, the total assets of its central bank, the Bank

GRAPH 12.4

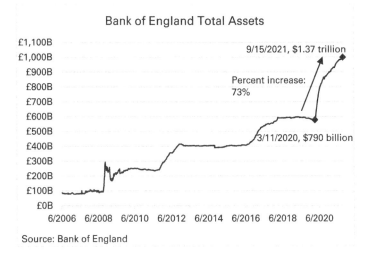

Bank of England Total Assets

9/15/2021, $1.37 trillion

Percent increase: 73%

3/11/2020, $790 billion

Source: Bank of England

GRAPH 12.5

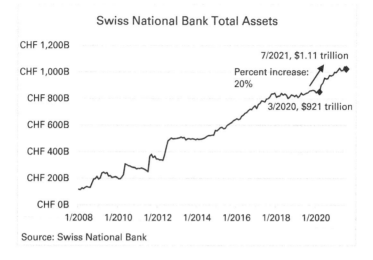

Swiss National Bank Total Assets

Source: Swiss National Bank

of Canada, had a striking rocket-like ascent beginning in 2020. Its assets multiplied more than four times in a year. Also remarkable, relative to the other central banks, is that the Bank of Canada actually reduced its assets in 2021, though they remain about four times as high as before the Covid panic.

GRAPH 12.6

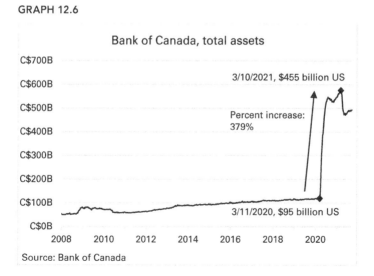

Bank of Canada, total assets

Source: Bank of Canada

In sum, the six central banks we have reviewed, as shown in Table 12.7, had total assets of over $26 trillion as of July 2021. Their vast growth since the $3.8 trillion of 2008, a multiple of about seven times, could have been predicted by no one then, and was not predicted by anyone, including themselves.

Table 12.8 compares these central banks' total assets per capita of their country's population, and the growth in this measure.

TABLE 12.7

Central Bank Total Asset Growth
in Billions of U.S. Dollars (Conversions)

	2008	2021	2021 as multiple of 2008
United States	$893	$8,079	9.0×
Eurozone	$1,714	$9,232	5.4×
Japan	$916	$6,472	7.1×
United Kingdom	$126	$1,338	10.7×
Switzerland	$148	$1,126	7.6×
Canada	$41	$380	9.3×
Total	$3,837	$26,627	6.9×

Sources: Board of Governors of the Federal Reserve System, European Central Bank, Bank of Japan, Bank of Canada, Bank of England, Swiss National Bank, Xe Currency Converter. The values shown are midyear estimates.

TABLE 12.8

Central Bank Total Assets per Capita
in U.S. Dollars (Conversions)

	2008	2020	2020 as multiple of 2008
United States	$2,936	$21,495	7.3×
Eurozone	$5,128	$21,312	4.2×
Japan	$7,149	$46,556	6.5×
United Kingdom	$2,031	$16,365	8.1×
Switzerland	$19,362	$119,737	6.2×
Canada	$1,227	$10,843	8.8×

Sources: Sources: World Bank, Board of Governors of the Federal Reserve System, European Central Bank, Bank of Japan, Bank of Canada, Bank of England, Swiss National Bank, Xe Currency Converter. The values shown are midyear estimates.

As central banks expand their assets while printing money, it is possible for them to direct credit to specific sectors of the economy. Naturally, the biggest beneficiary of the expanded credit is always the government (of which the central bank is a part), with its need for deficit financing. Ultimately, the government may also need depreciation of the currency to reduce the real burden of its expanded debt. But, particularly in the case of the Federal Reserve from 2009 to now (as we write), another specific target of its expansion is housing and housing finance.

In a fiat currency system there is, in principle, no limit to the kinds of assets a central bank can buy and monetize. We noted that the Swiss Central Bank holds equities, for example, as does the Bank of Japan. Of course, the authorizing laws may impose legal limits regarding what assets the central bank can hold. On the other hand, political forces may work toward an expansion of the kinds and amounts of assets the central bank will purchase, with a corresponding increase in risk. In the U.S. case, this has happened in housing investments.

We have already discussed the Federal Reserve's huge investment in mortgage securities and the implications of the rise of its mortgage holdings from an historically constant zero to $2.6 trillion in December 2021. Graph 8.3 is repeated here as Graph 12.9 to emphasize the fundamental shift in the role the Federal Reserve has defined for itself as it has become a dominant investor in mortgage assets, and the question of how this will develop in the future.

Bagehot and Nixon

We discussed the emergence of a Nixonian international monetary system in Chapter 6, and indeed the date of August 15, 1971 is crucial to understanding the power today's central banks have to apply Bagehot's theory in previously unimaginable fashion. On that Sunday evening, President Nixon came on television to announce an historic decision in his "Address to the Nation Outlining a New Economic Policy." Said Nixon to the nation, "The speculators have been waging an all-out war on the American

GRAPH 12.9

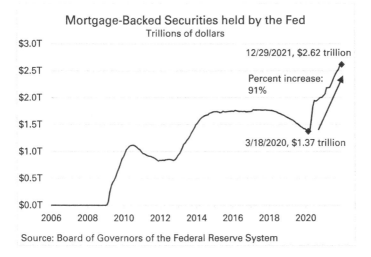

Mortgage-Backed Securities held by the Fed
Trillions of dollars

12/29/2021, $2.62 trillion

Percent increase: 91%

3/18/2020, $1.37 trillion

Source: Board of Governors of the Federal Reserve System

dollar. . . . Accordingly, I have directed [Treasury] Secretary Connolly to suspend temporarily the convertibility of the dollar into gold."[12] The suspension of course turned out to be permanent. Today everybody considers it normal and almost nobody can even imagine the slightest possibility of reversing it.

Nixon had thereby put the economic and financial world into a new era. By his decision to have the American government renege on its commitment to redeem dollars held by foreign governments for gold—to "close the gold window," as is said—he created a fundamentally changed international monetary system. In this new system, the system of today, the whole world runs on pure fiat currencies, none of which is redeemable in gold or anything else, except more paper currency or more accounting entries on the central banks' books. The central banks thereby became and remain free to print as much of their own currency as they and the government of which they are a part like.

This was a very big change indeed and highly controversial at the time. The ability of governments to redeem dollars for gold was unambiguously required by the International Bretton Woods agreement, negotiated in 1944 to define the post-World War II monetary order, approved by Congress and signed into U.S. law in 1945. But on August 15, 1971, as nicely summed up by economist Benn Steil:

> The Bretton Woods monetary system was finished. Though the bond between money and gold had been fraying for nearly sixty years, it had throughout most of the world and two and a half millennia of history been one that had only been severed as a temporary expedient in times of crisis. This time was different. The dollar was in essence the last ship moored to gold, with all the rest of the world's currencies on board, and the United States was cutting the anchor and sailing off for good.[13]

Nobody at the time knew how it would turn out.

Now, half a century later, we are entirely accustomed to the post-Bretton Woods fiat currency world. In this sense, in the United States and around the world, indeed, we are all Nixonians now. How has it turned out?

First of all, as we have been exploring, being in a fiat currency world is extremely useful for central banks and governments when they must confront a financial crisis—or a combined pandemic-political-economic-financial crisis including a financial market panic, as in March 2020.

But we must also consider that when the crisis has passed, we are still faced with the Cincinnatian Problem. Wasn't it dangerous to remove the discipline Bretton Woods provided against excessive money creation and inflationary credit expansion? The end of Bretton Woods, which solved an immediate dollar crisis, was followed over the next decade by the Great Inflation of the 1970s, with its disastrous consequences. Currently, we find that central banks, including the Federal Reserve, with a clear conscience commit themselves to "inflation targets" which actually mean perpetual inflation, instead of striving for stable prices. Without saying so directly, they promise to depreciate without limit the currency they issue. When they speak of "price stability," they mean a constant rate of inflation.

The most fundamental proposition in economics and in finance is: *Nothing is free.* Everything comes with some cost, some trade-off. Central bank hyper-money-printing and government deficits financed by monetization are not free either. Among their costs was bound to be rising inflation. And so it has transpired.

As we write, political and economic attention is rightly focused on the very high rate of consumer price inflation which emerged during 2021. This is in addition to the central bank-induced asset price inflation discussed in Chapter 5. By the end of 2021, with U.S. goods and services inflation running at 7 percent per year as measured by the Consumer Price Index—the highest inflation rate in almost four decades—it was judged unacceptable by all. Needless to say, such an inflation cuts real wages and robs savers of the purchasing power of their savings.

As we have seen, this inflationary result greatly surprised the Federal Reserve, whose forecasts for 2021 inflation were hopelessly low and wrong. Considering this contrast between forecast and outcome, we may reasonably ask whether central banks or governments can ever know what the follow-on effects of their interventions will be. We doubt it.

Professor Guido Hülsmann, speaking in 2021, described his view of the longer-term results of Nixon's 1971 decision in these colorful terms:

> All central bankers were suddenly free to print and lend as many dollars and pounds and francs and marks as they wished. . . . Nixon's decision led to an explosion of debt, public and private; to an unprecedented boom in real estate and financial markets; . . . to a mindboggling redistribution of incomes and wealth in favor of governments and the financial sector; and a pathetic dependence of the so-called financial industry on every whim of the central banks.[14]

Central banking to the max, as practiced in 2020 to finance the Covid crisis and continued in 2021, was made possible by President Nixon's decision in 1971. The fiat currency global monetary system he launched is so entrenched that most people can't imagine anything else. Similarly entrenched is the ability and determination of central banks to ride to the rescue of financial markets when needed.

Thus, for better and for worse, today's monetary world is both fully Nixonian and fully Bagehotian. This gives fiat currency central banks impressive power. In addition, as also discussed in Chapter 6, there is the looming possibility that, through central bank digital currencies, they could acquire vast new powers over economy-wide credit allocation and over individuals' private financial lives—one might even imagine the extreme case in which the central bank becomes the monopoly bank for the whole country, holding all consumer and business deposits, supplanting the private banking industry, and with its political agenda dominating the allocation of loans. This is a nightmare scenario for all believers in free markets and competition.

The world has not yet figured out how to solve the Cincinnatian Problem created by the massive interventions of central banks with fiat currencies, or how the advantages of their dramatic credit expandability can be matched by the disciplines and the checks and balances essential to a republic. So whatever the technological possibilities may be, it seems to us quite clear that central banks should not be made even more powerful than they already are. Their power has been amply demonstrated by central banking to the max in Covid times.

CHAPTER 13

Reflections on the Surprises
of the Covid Crisis

T̲o̲ ̲s̲u̲m̲m̲a̲r̲i̲z̲e̲:
The year 2020 brought a financial panic and crisis that *nobody* predicted. We were all surprised—again. The financial crisis arose from the unanticipated interaction of the Covid pandemic, fear, collapsing asset prices, a classic dash for cash, radical government actions in response to the pandemic, a resulting severe economic contraction, and extreme financial uncertainty.

The remarkable scale and breadth of the government and central bank interventions to stabilize the panic and finance the crisis, applying Bagehot's theory to the maximum extent, were memorable. These interventions worked in the short term. Their longer-term costs, including the emergence of high consumer price inflation and record government debt, heavily monetized by the central banks, continue as very challenging financial effects of the Covid crisis. The 2021 inflation of 7 percent surprised the Federal Reserve, which both caused it *and* wrongly predicted the year's inflation at 1.8 percent. In 2020, Charles Goodhart and Manoj Pradhan predicted a 2021 inflation rate of 5 to 10 percent, and were right, so they weren't surprised,[1] and Lawrence Summers wrote in February 2021 that "There is a chance . . . [of] inflationary pressures of a kind we have not seen in a generation,"[2] so he wasn't surprised either, but lots of "experts" were.

Such long-term costs again demonstrate the most fundamental of all economic principles: *Nothing is free.*

177

The interventions supported expansive asset price inflations and surprising super-bull markets in equities, cryptocurrencies, and houses, which took off in mid-2020 and ran through 2021, feeding on the negative real interest rates created by the Federal Reserve. At the end of 2021, the real interest rate on savings accounts was negative 7 percent.

Cryptocurrency super-bull markets surprised conservative financial thinkers who kept insisting that "there is nothing there," but the prices went sky high anyway, although with extremely volatile up and down moves. The central banks of the world are working toward issuing their own version of cryptocurrencies, that is, central bank digital currencies. This may produce the wonderfully ironic outcome that the cryptocurrency movement, intended to attack central banks' power, may end up making them even more powerful than before.

Runaway inflation in house prices took them far over their previous housing bubble peak of 2006, and they were still rising rapidly as 2021 ended. The Federal Reserve, in a fashion that would have been exceptionally surprising to its founders, stoked this price inflation by acting as the nation's dominant investor in residential mortgages, pushing its mortgage securities portfolio up to $2.6 trillion. This kept mortgage interest rates abnormally low. Although mortgage interest rates were rising in early 2022, for them to reach a historically normal level, they would have to rise a lot. This would reverse the path of house prices, should it happen.

The Covid crisis caused banks to book huge loan loss reserves in 2020; they then reversed them in 2021, deeming the reserves unnecessary. Had governments and central banks not intervened so forcefully, however, the big loss reserves might have been necessary after all.

Politicians used the excuse (or opportunity) of the Covid crisis to enact a massive bailout of insolvent multiemployer pension plans. The utter lack of any accompanying reform of these plans was, if not a surprise, still a major disappointment and a mistake. This bailout proved once again that "implicit" government guarantees—of the Pension Benefit Guarantee Corporation, in this case—are in fact real guarantees when push comes to shove. According to its chartering statute, the PBGC was supposed to stand on its own financially, but it couldn't and didn't. This was definitely not a surprise.

Many public employee pension plans continue to have giant deficits. If these deficits are ever funded, it would be a surprise. In Illinois and Chicago, it would be an especially big surprise.

The Covid crisis made the stunning losses of the government's student loan program grow even larger. If student loans could be converted from a loss-making to a break-even program, it would be as big a surprise as fixing Illinois' and Chicago's pension plans.

The Federal Reserve balance sheet grew to $8.9 trillion. Nobody predicted that. The combined assets of the Federal Reserve and five other important central banks grew to a total of $26 trillion. Ditto. Perhaps that will prove to have been the peak, until the next crisis.

Overall, the events and surprises of 2020 and 2021 reemphasize the profound truth that the financial and economic future is not only unknown, but unknowable—as it was for those who tried so diligently to foresee it in 2019, and as it is for us now.

How Deadly Has the Pandemic Been?

The global spread of the Covid pandemic was of course a surprise to most people, although predictions of the possibility or probability of such pandemics were well-known to scientists. That the pandemic brought a financial crisis, however, was a complete surprise.

Any crisis and the risks associated with it, such as death from Covid, can be thought of in absolute numbers or in percentages. Both measures are relevant and equally true, although they may generate different impressions.

The media always emphasize the absolute numbers, which have more immediate impact on human emotions, including fear, of which Covid generated plenty. Graph 13.1 shows the total reported deaths to date from Covid in the United States, which through December 2021 were 820,000.

But to calculate the odds, you have to consider the percentages. Graph 13.2 shows the total deaths as a percent of the U.S. population. Through December 2021, this was 0.25 percent.

GRAPH 13.1

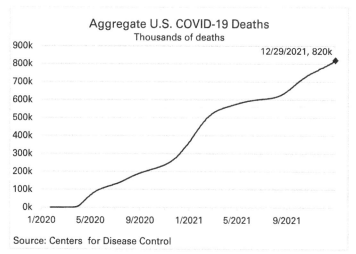

Aggregate U.S. COVID-19 Deaths
Thousands of deaths

12/29/2021, 820k

Source: Centers for Disease Control

GRAPH 13.2

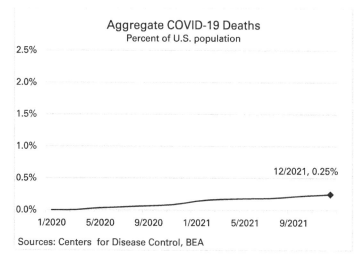

Aggregate COVID-19 Deaths
Percent of U.S. population

12/2021, 0.25%

Sources: Centers for Disease Control, BEA

By way of comparison, the 1918–19 influenza pandemic is said to have killed 50 million people or about 2.5 percent of a world population of 2 billion at the time. Even that was not in the league of the Black Death, which killed an estimated one-third of the population of Europe and has provoked guesses of deaths of from 5 percent to 40 percent of the worldwide population.[3]

But Covid is certainly bad enough, as was its intertwined financial and economic crisis. As we write, Covid is not over, with its Omicron variant spreading, and further dangerous mutations perhaps in store. Unless they are particularly deadly, however, it seems they will no longer come as such a big surprise.

But the future will doubtless bring more big financial surprises.

The Next Financial Crisis?

The great financial historian, Charles Kindleberger, observed in the 1970s that over four centuries, history showed there was a financial crisis approximately every ten years. His observation has continued to hold in every decade since his classic *Manias, Panics, and Crashes* was first published in 1978. Such crises have indeed erupted in their turn in the 1980s, 1990s, 2000s, 2010s, and in 2020.

As Paul Volcker so memorably and so wittily put it, "About every ten years, we have the biggest crisis in 50 years."

What might cause the *next* crisis in this long, recurring series? We are back to asking the same question the authors were pondering in December 2019, as described in the first paragraph of this book.

We can imagine several possibilities. Can you add others as you guess about the financial future, Insightful Reader? Here are our "next crisis" scenarios:

THE COST OF THE CINCINNATIAN PROBLEM

We have discussed the Cincinnatian Doctrine: that emergency interventions need to be withdrawn when the crisis is over; and the accompanying Cincinnatian Problem: that it is hard for central banks to "take away the punch bowl" when the time has come, and easy to keep the party going too long.

It is possible that by failing to follow the Cincinnatian Doctrine—by continuing the radical money printing too long and thereby promoting the global Everything Bubble—the Federal Reserve and the international club of central banks have themselves laid the groundwork for the next financial crisis. If this is so, they will have all gotten it wrong together (after first all getting it right together to address the panic). This reflects the fact that central bank decisions are subject to fundamental uncertainty and therefore to cognitive and behavioral herding.

It has been asserted that "Central banks have become slaves to the bubbles that they blow" to explain their continuing to fill up the punch bowl too many times.[4] Whether or not we think that is the case, the principal central banks have together managed to create a gigantic asset price inflation and also an unacceptable and threatening consumer price inflation.

Given the inflation that is upon us, interest rates presumably must rise significantly, and then asset prices will fall. That will happen in a setting of stretched asset valuations and high levels of debt. As asset prices fall, formerly profitable speculation, especially leveraged speculation, will be punished. This could include a selloff caused by a loss of faith in speculative assets like the now large cryptocurrency market. As Bagehot wrote, "Every great crisis reveals the excessive speculations of many houses which no one before suspected." Or in Warren Buffet's more homely metaphor, when the tide goes out, they will be found to have been swimming naked.

If, under this pressure, the Everything Bubble of our time then implodes, the next crisis would be upon us and the cycle of elastic currency and bailouts will almost certainly begin anew.

A HOUSING COLLAPSE AGAIN

We return to the particularly notable inflation that has, once again, occurred in the prices in the giant market for houses. As

2021 ended, these were rising in the U.S. at an unsustainable rate, but this is also a global problem, with many countries—20 by one count—facing extreme house price increases. Colorfully summarized by one commenter, "This is now a global property bubble of epic proportions never before seen by man or beast and it has entrapped more [central banks] than just the Fed."[5]

House prices depend on high leverage and are therefore very interest rate sensitive. Should U.S. mortgage interest rates rise to historically normal levels, say 5 percent or 6 percent, let alone if they should go higher, required monthly payments on mortgages would rise steeply, the price that the same house buyer can afford would correspondingly fall steeply, and house prices would follow downward. House price appreciation would once again become house price depreciation. Highly leveraged recent buyers would find themselves "under water," owing more on the mortgage than the current market price of the house. Refinancing activity, and cash-out refinancing in particular, would shrink. Taking a global view, this could be accompanied by a collapse of real estate finance in China.

Overpriced, overleveraged real estate is a frequent culprit in financial crises. Perhaps the latest house price bubble will also implode if faced with much higher interest rates. Even though, historically speaking, these interest rates would be moderate, they would be very high compared to the suppressed rates which are the basis of recent valuations.

A PURELY MALICIOUS MACRO-HACK
OF THE FINANCIAL SYSTEM

We keep learning about how vulnerable to hacking, especially by state-sponsored hackers, even the most "secure" computer systems are. Here we are considering not a hack to make money or collect blackmail, or a hack for spying, but a purely malicious hack with the goal of creating financial destruction and panic, to cripple the United States by bringing down our exceptionally complex and totally computer-dependent financial system.

Imagine macro-hackers attacking with the same destructive motivation as the 9/11 terrorists. Suppose when they strike, payment and trading systems can't function, there are no market prices, no one can find out the balance of their accounts or the value of their positions, and no one can know who is broke or who solvent.

AN ELECTRICITY SYSTEM FAILURE

The financial system is completely dependent on electricity. Imagine a failure, similar to the financial system macro-hack scenario, resulting from an attack maliciously carried out to bring down the national electricity system. Should that happen, in addition to candles and firewood, it would certainly be a good idea to have some paper money in your leather (not digital) wallet, and maybe some actual gold coins. Bank accounts and cryptocurrencies, even central bank digital currencies, would not be working too well.

THE *NEXT* PANDEMIC

It feels like we have survived the Covid pandemic and are becoming resigned to living with this virus and its variants. Even with the Delta and then the Omicron variants, we are certainly less frightened than at the peak of intense fear and the lockdowns in 2020. The free fall of panicked financial markets of that time has become history until the next crisis.

Could that come with the *next* deadly pandemic? We discovered that to combat a pandemic, governments can close down whole sectors of the economy and cause massive unemployment and economic and financial disruption. They could do it again.

A new pandemic might be much more deadly than Covid, bringing more draconian political reactions and renewed extreme uncertainty, and triggering a new financial crisis.

A MAJOR WAR

By far the most important financial events of all are big wars.

The outbreak of the First World War set off a financial panic.

The warring governments financed themselves by printing money and created runaway inflation. The war left behind huge, intractable debt that lasted until the many sovereign defaults of the 1930s.

In the Second World War, "The currencies and debts of Germany, Japan, and Italy, as well as those of China and a number of other countries, were quickly and totally destroyed, while those of most winners of the war were slowly but still substantially depreciated."[6]

Financing the Vietnam War helped set off the Great Inflation of the 1970s and the ensuing financial crises of the 1980s.

Imagine the financial reaction if a war between major powers happened again in the 21st century. We would like to think that is not possible, just as the once-famous book, Norman Angell's *The Great Illusion*, published in 1910, very rationally argued that a 20th century war among European powers would be so economically costly that it would not happen. In the event, the First World War's economic cost bankrupted the principal European countries involved (not to mention all its other terrible costs), but it happened nonetheless.

A student of geopolitical strategy has described China as "Germany in 1913," and the distinguished scholar Graham Allison wrote, "A disastrous war between the United States and China in the decades ahead is not just possible, but much more likely than most of us are willing to allow."[7] Discussion of possible war between the U.S. and China resulting from a Chinese invasion of Taiwan became fairly common in 2021.

Would anybody really be crazy enough to start a war between China and the United States? We all certainly hope not, but we should remember that such a war did already occur: most of the Korean War consisted of battles between the Chinese and the American armies. "The Chinese viewed Korea as a great success," one historian wrote, and Mao "had shrewdly understood the domestic political benefits of having his country at war with the Americans."[8]

A war with China could have a drastic impact because of the large amount of investment by each of these countries in the other's economy. The Congressional Research Service estimates that in 2019, China held $1.5 trillion in U.S. securities, including U.S. Treasury securities, and the American Enterprise Institute estimated in July 2021 that U.S. investment in China exceeded $1 trillion. Imagine if, for example, as part of a military confrontation with China, China were to dump all of its U.S. securities into the market and expropriate all U.S. investments in China to exacerbate the financial impact on the United States of any military confrontation. The same type of extensive economic interdependence that now characterizes the U.S. and China was, according to the theory of Norman Angell, what made major 20th-century wars impossible. What if his theory is wrong again?

If a big-powers war did happen again, it would be a crisis, needless to say, with perhaps a financial panic thrown in. This is particularly so because a war with any of our current adversaries, including China or Russia, could well involve hacking and cybersecurity attacks on our financial and other infrastructure of the types mentioned earlier. These adversaries are certainly capable of such attacks and, in fact, have already engaged in hacks against U.S. entities and systems.

As seen from early 2022, Russian President Putin's provocations towards Ukraine bring to mind troubling resemblances to Hitler's demands on Czechoslovakia in the 1930s. While Russia may be less powerful than the Soviet Union before its collapse, it is still a major nuclear power, its leadership is aggressive, and the threat of a war with Russia is also not inconceivable.

A COMBINATION OF THE ABOVE

Of course, it could be a combination of any of the factors above that would lead to another financial crisis. The possible combinations and permutations are part of the inherent uncertainty.

WHAT NOBODY SEES COMING

Finally, the next financial crisis may erupt from none of the above and, like the Covid crisis, from what nobody sees coming—not the diligent students of systemic risk, nor central banks, nor financial stability committees, nor financial markets, nor anybody else, including, of course, the authors. In spite of all the looking downfield, so to speak, the financial system may once more be the quarterback who takes a blind side hit for a big sack. In short, we will have been surprised again.

You will have seen, Perceptive Reader, that this brings us back to the ideas and ironies of Chapter 1.

More Uncertainty

W E F I N I S H E D the manuscript of this book in early February, 2022. Now in mid-May, as it moves toward publication, we have had three more months of post-Covid panic history, which gives us a last chance for an update. These three months have brought new surprises, plenty of financial volatility, and undiminished uncertainty.

At the end of Chapter 13, we considered wars as the most important financial events and the possibility of a war involving major powers, noting that "the threat of a war with Russia is also not inconceivable." Less than a month later, Russian tanks were rolling over the Ukrainian border, and the type of European war that many had thought no longer possible and a matter only for history, was once again grim reality.

"Get to the end of last year [2021]," investment adviser David Kotok recently wrote. "In December, did you think we would see a shooting war in February?"[1] We would bet, Excellent Reader, that you didn't. As for the authors, while we highlighted the possibility, we didn't predict it.

Another surprise, for observers as well as for the Russian leadership, was that the invasion did not turn into an easy Russian victory. Instead, the Ukrainian forces, under their own inspiring leadership and with material assistance from other countries, put up and, as we write, continue a stout defense.

The United States does not have soldiers in the shooting war but has waged an economic and financial world war with Russia, in addition to supplying money, war materiel, and intelligence to Ukraine. In Chapter 6, we discussed the "weaponization" of the dollar. The U.S. has organized an intense weaponization of the dollar-based international financial system to seize assets, including central bank reserves, and prevent transactions involving Russian entities.

Some have argued that in the long run this will work against the dollar's role as the world's dominant reserve currency by making central banks suspicious of how, in a dollar system, the American government has "brandished" its special power to financially punish others and expropriate their reserves.[2] Will this push other countries to non-dollar reserve strategies? Might they turn to cryptocurrency or commodity-based currencies to avoid the threat of this U.S. monetary power? The Russians are developing a digital ruble, and by February 2022 there was speculation that Russia might use this form of cryptocurrency or the digital yuan of its ally, China, to evade U.S. sanctions.[3] If the Russia-Ukraine War were to result in a developing threat to the dollar system, it might tilt the Federal Reserve and the Treasury to active pursuit of a Federal Reserve digital dollar to support the dollar's global role.

In February 2022, we saw Canada weaponize its domestic financial system to punish protesting truckers by blocking their bank accounts and their ability to use their own money. This kind of act is what is feared, as we also discussed in Chapter 6, from the Chinese use of its central bank digital currency for authoritarian control of the population. In the U.S. and many other countries the debate about central bank digital currencies continues, including among other issues their potential use for political surveillance and control.[4]

High inflation, having completely surprised the Federal Reserve in 2021, has continued in 2022, running as we write at the disastrous rate of over 8 percent.

"Inflation is back," said Agustin Carstens, General Manager of the Bank for International Settlements, in April 2022, adding that "We may be on the cusp of a new inflationary era" and "almost

60% of [advanced economies] currently have year-on-year inflation above 5%."[5]

Having given up on its former rationalization that the inflation was "transitory," the Federal Reserve belatedly set out to try to control it. In May 2022, it raised the federal funds target rate by 0.5 percent. This was much discussed as a large increase, but it brought the target range to only 0.75 percent to 1 percent—still an exceptionally low interest rate. The Federal Reserve has promised more increases, but with inflation at 8 percent, the real federal funds rate is about negative 7 percent. Short-term interest rates, although they no longer round to zero, are still far below where a free money market would set them, and they are still inflationary.

Rates on savings and money market fund accounts remain miniscule, so the real yield to savers is about negative 8 percent. In other words, so far in 2022, the government is effectively confiscating through depreciation of the dollar about 8 percent of savers' nest eggs per year. On the other hand, savings accounts are at least not going down in nominal terms, unlike the dropping prices of stocks, bonds, and cryptocurrencies as we write.

A notable exception to near zero interest rates on savings is the Series I U.S. Savings Bond. This bond pays the holder whatever the recent increase in the Consumer Price Index is over six-month periods—as we write, it is paying a rate of 9.6 percent interest, a notable improvement. Unfortunately, the Treasury allows you to buy only $10,000 of these savings bonds per person per year. We can imagine the Treasury officials vigorously saying to each other, "We can't allow ordinary savers to protect themselves against inflation!"

Long-term interest rates have risen in 2022, with the ten-year Treasury note yield rising to over 3 percent. But from a historical view, that is still a low rate. The Federal Reserve has now stopped increasing its portfolio of long-term Treasury securities, reducing the downward pressure it has exerted on the interest rates of these securities and allowing them to rise toward a market level.

The Federal Reserve also, very belatedly, stopped increasing its investment in mortgage securities in March, and told the market it will begin to let them run off beginning in June.[6] In Chapter 8, we raised the question, "If Mortgage Rates Go Back to Normal, What Then?" We suggested that normal might mean 5 or 6 percent on 30-year fixed-rate mortgages, instead of the 3 percent of 2021. By May, mortgage rates have already risen to about 5 ½ percent. This means interest expense on the same sized mortgage for the same priced house has increased by about 80 percent. That will make many houses unaffordable for many prospective buyers and therefore must, we guess, moderate house price inflation. However, as we write, house prices are still rising rapidly. Stay tuned.

In Chapter 13, we wrote, "Given the inflation that is upon us, interest rates must rise significantly and then asset prices will fall. . . . Formerly profitable speculation, especially leveraged speculation, will be punished. This could include a selloff caused by a lack of faith in the now large cryptocurrency market."

So far, three months later, the Everything Bubble we discuss in the book does seem to be deflating. Year-to-date investment returns up to May 10, 2022, include: Dow Jones Industrial Average, −12 percent; Nasdaq Composite Index, −26 percent; S&P 500 Index, −17 percent; Long-term Treasury bonds,[7] −20 percent; Bitcoin, −25 percent; ARK Innovation ETF, a symbol of the tech stock super-bull market, −58 percent.

ARK Innovation has losses this year in 34 of its 35 positions as we write; the only exception is its money market fund account.[8] Various highly speculative and faddish stocks are down 60 percent or more from their highs.

Coming to cryptocurrencies, an index of the top 500 digital assets has shrunk 50 percent from its November 2021 peak. Correspondingly, from its November peak, the price of Bitcoin was down about 54 percent. An index of the top five cryptocurrencies excluding Bitcoin was off 70 percent from the recent high.[9]

On May 11, 2022, the stablecoin Terra USD, designed to maintain a steady price of one dollar, dropped to a low of 30 cents, later recovering to about 80 cents, then on May 12 falling again to as low as 8 cents—a long way from a dollar and not so stable. The resulting *Wall Street Journal* headlines were "Terra USD Craters in Crypto Rout" and "Stablecoin Crash Shakes Crypto: 'Run on the Bank.'"[10] Terra USD's linked sister cryptocurrency, Luna, was reported to have lost 99.7 percent of its value.[11] Is that the cryptocurrency craze unraveling or just inevitable creative destruction?

The panic in this cryptocurrency market suggests there will be increasing political will to regulate cryptocurrency markets more stringently, particularly for stablecoins. In Chapter 6, we discussed the recommendation of the President's Working Group that stablecoin issuers must be regulated banks and suggested that such a draconian regulatory solution might make these companies unprofitable. In the meantime, other regulatory regimes have been suggested. Two regulatory regimes that are similar to one another have been suggested, one by Senator Toomey in a discussion draft of a Senate bill and one by the European Union in proposed legislation, "Markets in Crypto Assets," which is currently wending its way through the European Union's labyrinthine approval process.[12] Both proposals would require stablecoin issuers to obtain a license, but not necessarily a bank license. They also would require clear disclosures about reserve assets and redemption policies and would provide for capital, liquidity, and governance standards. Most importantly, they would require audited financial statements.

These two proposals appear to remedy the most egregious problems with stablecoins while giving them a fair chance to be profitable in a regulated environment. We do not know how much of enduring value the cryptocurrency industry has to offer, but we believe that regulators should not only protect investors against fraud and ensure that risks are disclosed but, within this framework, allow possibly innovative technologies to compete so that the market can decide whether they succeed or fail.

We turn to central banks' own balance sheets. As discussed in Chapter 12, the Swiss National Bank includes equities in its large investment portfolio. This central bank reported a $33 billion loss for the first quarter of 2022, caused by a $37 billion loss on its non-Swiss franc equities and bonds. To its credit, the bank marks investments to market value for its financial statements.

To find the market value of the Federal Reserve's massive investments, in contrast, you have to search far into the dense footnotes to the financial statements. We estimate that year-to-date 2022, through April, the Federal Reserve probably suffered about $650 billion in unrealized, mark-to-market losses on its mortgage securities and bonds. Since they had an unrealized gain of about $128 billion on December 31, 2021, this suggests that net, the Fed is down well over $500 billion on a mark-to-market basis. Quite a number. Compare it to their capital of $41 billion.

Almost all economists assure us that it does not matter at all if the central bank is insolvent on a mark-to-market basis, and they may be right. Still, we wonder if the Federal Reserve investment managers actually planned to lose that much money.

We sum up the preceding observations as follows: the air is now coming out of the great Everything Bubble that the Federal Reserve and the other major central banks intentionally inflated. Of course, what comes after that is uncertain, as always.

Discussing the deep problems of public pension plans in Chapter 10, we pointed out that the robust investment gains of the 2020–21 bull markets could not continue forever. As we write, the current market corrections in both stocks and bonds are reducing the value of pensions' assets, while at the same time, since many public pensions feature cost of living adjustments, the high inflation is increasing the plans' liabilities. About half of all states link pension benefits in some fashion to the Consumer Price Index.[13] "State and City Retirement Funds Face Mounting Losses,"[14] was the May *Wall Street Journal* headline. We repeat our conclusion that the huge public pension deficits and their stress on state and municipal budgets are not going away.

Student loans have continued to be a hot political and hopeless financial topic. The Biden administration extended the costly period of no required payments through August 2022. The administration is under political pressure to announce a generalized forgiveness of student loans, a step of dubious legality, which, as we discussed in Chapter 11, would create enormous expense for the taxpayers. Financial advisers are telling borrowers not to pay their student loans, even if they have the cash available.[15] Should it occur, blanket loan forgiveness would be the final proof of the utter failure of federal student loans as a lending program.

Among other unexpected developments of 2022, first quarter real GDP fell at a rate of 1.4 percent. "The contraction caught nearly every Wall Street economist by surprise."[16] Needless to say, no one should be surprised by economic forecasters being surprised. Many commentators now wonder whether the U.S. is headed for stagflation, that is, the combination of poor economic growth and high inflation. Maybe.

IN 2020, 2021, and thus far in 2022, we have often enough been surprised again. As we reflect on these events, we are in a context of war, economic war, dollar weaponization, high inflation, rising interest rates, deflation of the Everything Bubble, reversal of central banks' policy, continuing pension fund deficits, huge losses from student loans, worries about stagflation, and, lurking worldwide, the Covid virus and its variants still with us.

What next? In a nice turn of phrase, one financial analyst said in early May that we have a "thick stew of uncertainties."[17] The editors of the *Financial Times* at greater length opined that "This is a time of incredible complexity: each week has thrown up a new shock or revealed that the problems we saw coming were bigger than we thought. . . . The staccato of recent crises has created astonishing uncertainty."[18] Well, yes, but not uncertainty more astonishing than that of the Covid panic in March 2020.

The weather forecast for the financial and economic future always remains the same: "Foggy."

APPENDIX

Your Own Update

	Covid panic (3-31-20)	Manuscript completed (2-10-22)	Epilogue written (5-12-22)	When you read this book (date: _____)
Inflation Rate (CPI year over year)	2.3%	7.5%	8.3%	_____
Dow Jones Industrial Ave.	21,219	35,241	31,730	_____
Nasdaq Composite Index	7,700	14,186	11,371	_____
3-month Treasury Yield	0.11%	0.42%	0.97%	_____
10-year Treasury Yield	0.70%	2.03%	2.82%	_____
30-year Mortgage Interest Rate (Mortgage Bankers Assn.)	3.47%	3.83%	5.53%	_____
Bitcoin Price	$6,439	$43,565	$29,048	_____
TerraUSD Price	Not yet introduced	$1.00	$0.18	_____
Major War?	No	No	Yes	_____
Total Assets of the Federal Reserve	$5.3 T	$8.9 T	$8.9 T	_____

Notes

Chapter 1 · Surprised Again!

1. FSOC was established by the Dodd-Frank Act of 2010 to oversee systemic financial risk. Among its members are the heads of all the major federal financial agencies, including the Treasury Department, Federal Reserve, Securities and Exchange Commission, Comptroller of the Currency, Federal Deposit Insurance Corporation, Commodity Futures Trading Commission, and representatives of various state regulatory agencies.

2. Alex J. Pollock, *Finance and Philosophy—Why We're Always Surprised*, 2018.

3. "Yellen: I Don't See a Financial Crisis Occurring 'In Our Lifetimes,'" *U.S. News*, June 27, 2017.

4. "Memo to Morgan Stanley," *Grant's Interest Rate Observer*, Sept. 20, 2013.

5. Michael S. Derby and Kristina Peterson, "Is the Fed Doing Enough—or Too Much—to Aid Recovery?" *Wall Street Journal*, Jan. 6, 2013.

6. William R. White, comments at a conference on *The 2008 Global Financial Crisis in Retrospect*, 2018; and "Conducting Monetary Policy in a Complex, Adaptive Economy: Past Mistakes and Future Possibilities," *Credit and Capital Markets*, Feb. 2017, p. 220.

7. Claudio Borio and William White, "Whither monetary and financial stability? The implications of evolving policy regimes," Bank for International Settlements, Feb. 2004.

8. Henry M. Paulson, *On the Brink*, 2010. See the set of quotations from this book in Alex J. Pollock, "On Being Surprised (While Treasury Secretary)," *AEIdeas*, Nov. 18, 2010.

9. John Kay and Mervyn King, *Radical Uncertainty*, 2020, pp. 14, 16.

10. Morgan Housel, "The Big Lessons from History,"*CollaborativeFund. com*, Nov. 12, 2020.

11. Office of Financial Research, Annual Report to Congress 2020.

12. Interviewed by Matthew C. Klein in "The Coronavirus Pandemic Wasn't a Black Swan Event. Why We Must Prepare for More Outbreaks." *Barron's*, Dec. 7, 2020.

13. John Maynard Keynes, *The General Theory of Employment*, 1937.

14. *Grant's Interest Rate Observer*, April 17, 2020.

15. Mieszko Mazur, Man Dang, and Miguel Vega, "COVID-19 and the March 2020 stock market crash. Evidence from S&P 1500," July 9, 2020.

16. Tyler Durden, "I've Never, Ever, Ever Seen Anything Like This Before," *Zero Hedge*, March 26, 2020.

17. Paul McCaffrey, "Annie Duke and Morgan Housel: Three Tools for Navigating Risk and Uncertainty," *CFAInstitute.org*, June 6, 2020.

18. See Pollock, *Finance and Philosophy*, Chapter 16, "The Cincinnatian Doctrine."

19. Gwynn Guilford and Sarah Chaney Cambon, "U.S. Economy's Rebound is 'Without Historical Parallel,'" *Wall Street Journal*, June 3, 2021, p. A8.

20. Douglas Carr, "How Deficit 'Stimulus' Supercharged Inflation," *National Review*, Dec. 2021.

21. AEI Housing Center, "AEI housing market indicators, December 2021," *AEIdeas*, Jan. 4, 2022.

22. Danilo Cascaldi-Garcia et al., "What is Certain about Uncertainty?" Federal Reserve Board, July 2020.

Chapter 2 · The Panic of 2020

1. "GDP Growth—Second quarter of 2020," Statistics and Data Directorate, OECD, Aug. 26, 2020.

2. "Recent Disruptions and Potential Reforms in the U. S. Treasury Market: A Staff Progress Report" (Department of the Treasury, Board of Governors of the Federal Reserve System, Federal Reserve Bank of N.Y., SEC, CFTC), Nov. 8, 2021, p. 23.

3. 2020 Annual Report, Financial Stability Oversight Council (FSOC), p. 44.

4. Ibid., p. 43.

5. Ibid., p. 17.

6. Ibid., p. 19.

7. Ibid.

8. Ibid., p. 75

9. "Creditors Foreclose on Another Mall of Simon Property Group, Face Massive Loss," *Wolf Street*, July 21, 2021.

10. 2020 FSOC Annual Report, p. 62.

11. Jann Swanson, "Forbearances Drop Below 1 Million, Exits Slow," *Mortgage News Daily*, Dec. 21, 2021.

Chapter 3 · Elastic Currency to the Rescue

1. Paul Tucker, "The Repertoire of Official Sector Interventions in the Financial System: Last Resort Lending, Market-Making and Capital," speech given at the Bank of Japan 2009 International Conference, May 28, 2009.
2. Office of Financial Research (OFR), Annual Report to Congress 2020, p. 17.
3. Andrew Keshner, "COVID-19 has caused real financial pain. So why did consumer bankruptcies drop in 2020?" *MarketWatch*, Jan. 14, 2021.

Chapter 4 · The Run on Prime Money Market Funds

1. "Money Market Fund Assets," Investment Company Institute, Jan. 27, 2022.
2. "Global Money Market Fund Flows Dashboard: 2Q21," Fitch Ratings, Sept. 1, 2021.
3. Justin Baer, "Money Funds Anxious Over Rules," *Wall Street Journal*, Aug. 28, 2021.
4. Paul J. Davies, "Money-Market Funds Buckled in Two Crises in a Row. Regulators Look to Fix Them Again," *Wall Street Journal*, July 19, 2021.
5. See Pollock, *Finance and Philosophy*, Chapter 3, "Bubbles and 'Liquidity.'"
6. Report of the President's Working Group on Financial Markets, "Overview of Recent Events and Potential Reform Options for Money Market Funds," Dec. 22, 2020.
7. Ibid., p. 19.
8. "Money Market Fund Reforms," Securities and Exchange Commission, Rel. No. IC-34441 Dec. 15, 2021.
9. "Policy Proposals to Enhance Money Market Fund Resilience," Financial Stability Board, June 30, 2021, p. 21.
10. Ibid., p. 36.

Chapter 5 · A Second Surprise: The Amazing 2020–21 Market Boom

1. Jeremy Grantham, "Let the Wild Rumpus Begin," GMO Viewpoints, Jan. 20, 2022, p. 7.
2. David Hodari, "Oil Demand Set to Rise In Shift From Coal, Gas," *Wall Street Journal*, Oct. 15, 2021.

3. International Energy Agency, *Gas Market Report* Q1 2022.

4. John Hussman, quoted in "Strategic Investment Potpourri," *Thoughts from the Frontline,* June 19, 2021.

Chapter 6 · Cryptocurrencies: An Assault on Central Banks or Their New Triumph?

1. F. A. Hayek, *New Studies in Philosophy, Politics, Economics, and the History of Ideas,* 1978, pp. 218 ff.

2. Ben Schreckinger, "A crypto breakthrough? Western states consider taking digital currency," *Politico,* Feb. 1, 2022.

3. Raphael Auer et al., "Central bank digital currencies: motives, economic implications and the research frontier," Bank for International Settlements Working Papers No. 976, Nov. 2021, p. 6.

4. "Glitches, Fraud and High Fees Upset El Salvador's Chivo Wallet Users," *PYMNTS.com,* Oct 31, 2021.

5. David Gerard, "Bitcoin Failed in El Salvador. The President Says the Answer Is More Bitcoin," *foreignpolicy.com,* Dec. 6, 2021.

6. "IMF Wants Bitcoin Dropped as Currency," *Wall Street Journal,* Jan. 26, 2022.

7. Codruta Boar and Andreas Wehrli, "Ready, steady, go?—Results of the third BIS survey on central bank digital currency," Bank for International Settlements Papers No. 114, Jan. 2021, p. 6.

8. FSOC 2019 Annual Report, p. 96, citing CoinMarketCap.

9. https://coinmarketcap.com/charts/

10. See, e.g., United States Department of Justice, Report of the Attorney General's Cyber Digital Task Force, "Cryptocurrency Enforcement Framework," Oct. 2020.

11. Most stablecoins currently run on the Ethereum blockchain. Ethereum announced that it would be moving to a system where the right to validate transactions is based on how much cryptocurrency validators own and how long they have owned it. Under this system, transactions are checked by the validators who hold the most cryptocurrency on the blockchain, which presumably gives them a greater stake in honestly validating transactions. This might lead to greater security for blockchain transactions. Nonetheless, Ethereum has been hacked in the past, and it is not hard to believe that diligent hackers will find ways to penetrate it in the future.

12. Libra White Paper, June 18, 2019.

13. Ibid.

14. Tatiana Koffman, "Facebook's Libra White Paper is Now Live," *Forbes.com,* June 18, 2019.

15. Ray Dalio, *Principles for Dealing with the Changing World Order*, 2021, p. 479.

16. See, "In the Matter of Coinflip, Inc., d/b/a Derivabit, and Francisco Riordan," CFTC Docket No. 15-29, WL 5535736 (Sept. 17, 2015).

17. President's Working Group on Financial Markets, the Federal Deposit Insurance Corporation, and the Office of the Comptroller of the Currency, "Report on Stablecoins," Nov. 2021, p. 2.

18. Patrick J. Boot and Marysia Laskowski, "Wyoming Issues Second Crypto Bank Charter," *The National Law Review*, Nov. 10, 2020.

19. "Crypto's Boom Demands Response from Congress, Key Lawmaker Says," Bloomberg, Nov. 17, 2021.

20. A digital wallet is an account in a computer program that, in this case, stores a record of a cryptocurrency user's cryptocurrency holdings.

21. Oonagh McDonald, *Cryptocurrencies—Money, Trust and Regulation*, 2021, p. 117.

22. Ibid., Chapters 6 and 7.

23. "Libra Association: FINMA licensing process initiated," FINMA press release, April 16, 2020.

24. President's Working Group, "Report on Stablecoins."

25. Ibid., notes 7 and 8.

26. Lawrence H. White, "Should We Fear Stablecoins?" *Cato at Liberty*, June 24, 2021.

27. Elaine Yu and Joe Wallace, "China Declares Crypto Dealings Illegal," *Wall Street Journal*, Sept. 25–26, 2021.

28. James T. Areddy, "China Creates Its Own Digital Currency, a First for Major Economy," *Wall Street Journal*, April 5–6, 2021.

29. Ambrose Evans-Pritchard, "Bitcoin Fever is the Primrose Path to Digital Servitude," *The Telegraph*, May 28, 2021.

30. Areddy, "China," *Wall Street Journal*.

31. Triennial Central Bank Survey "Foreign exchange turnover in April 2019," Bank for International Settlements, Sept. 16, 2019.

32. Areddy, "China," *Wall Street Journal*.

33. David Sacks, "Countries in China's Belt and Road Initiative: Who's In and Who's Out," Council on Foreign Relations blog, March 24, 2021.

34. Ibid.

35. Testimony of Chairman Jerome Powell on the Semiannual Monetary Policy Report to the Congress before the Senate Committee on Banking, Housing and Urban Affairs Feb. 23, 2021.

36. "Money and Payments: The U.S. Dollar in the Age of Digital Transformation," Board of Governors of the Federal Reserve System, Jan. 2022, p. 1.

37. Ibid., pp. 14–16.

38. Ibid., pp. 17–20.

39. https://cbdctracker.org

Chapter 7 · Banks: Not Their Turn This Time

1. The "provision" for loan losses is the amount that a lender sets aside in each accounting period for future loan losses and is reflected as an expense in the lender's income statement for that period. The "reserve" for loan losses is the aggregate unspent amount that a lender has made available to cover loan losses and is reflected in the lender's balance sheet at the end of each accounting period.

2. Evan Lorenz, "Not banking on it," *Grant's Interest Rate Observer*, Oct. 15, 2021.

3. David Benoit and Orla McCaffrey, "Pandemic Profits Begin to Ebb at America's Biggest Banks," *Wall Street Journal*, Jan. 14, 2022.

4. "TARP" stood for the Troubled Asset Relief Program. Under it, the Treasury invested in the preferred stock of more than 700 banks. They also financed the bankrupt General Motors and Chrysler corporations through the program. The Treasury made a profit on the bank investments in total, but lost money on the auto companies.

5. 2020 FSOC Annual Report, p. 197.

6. 2019 FSOC Annual Report, p. 34.

7. Banks with total assets of $1 billion to $10 billion.

8. Federal Deposit Insurance Corporation, *Quarterly Banking Profile*, June 30, 2021.

9. Office of Financial Research, Annual Report to Congress 2020, p. 48.

10. *Quarterly Report on Household Debt and Credit (2021: Q4)*, Federal Reserve Bank of New York, Feb. 2022.

11. Congressional Research Service, *COVID-19 Impact on the Banking Industry: Conditions in the Second Quarter of 2020* (IN11500), Sept. 10, 2020.

12. The Consolidated Appropriations Act 2021, P.L. 116-260, Dec. 27, 2020.

13. Kathleen Day, "Sun Trust Got Caught in Reserves Tug of War," *Washington Post*, Dec. 29, 1998.

Chapter 8 · The Mortgage Market: Built on a Government Financial Triangle

1. S&P CoreLogic Case-Shiller U.S. National Home Price Index.

2. For a point of comparison, the Chinese mortgage loan market, which serves a population more than four times as big as the U.S., is estimated at $6 trillion in loans.

3. Howard led the interagency group that recommended to FSOC this rather modest recognition of economic reality.

4. See Alex J. Pollock, "Fannie and Freddie Are Obviously SIFIs," Testimony to the Senate Committee on Banking, Housing, and Urban Affairs, June 25, 2019.

5. Alex J. Pollock, Hashim Hamandi, and Ruth Leung, "Banking Credit System, 1970–2020," Office of Financial Research Blog, Jan. 6, 2021.

6. An important but little discussed fact is the relationship between marriage and home ownership. In 2015, the U.S. married homeownership rate was 78 percent, while not-married homeownership was 43 percent, comprising the overall rate of 63.5 percent. It is easy to think of reasons why owning your own home is more achievable and more important to you if you are married than if you are not, and the numbers bear this out. See Alex J. Pollock and Jay Brinkmann, "In Tracking Home Ownership, Marriage Matters," *RealClear Policy*, July 10, 2016; and Alex J. Pollock, "Homeownership Rates: It depends on whether you are married," *Housing Finance International*, Autumn 2016.

7. Ernest Fisher, *Housing Markets and Congressional Goals*, 1975, p. 103, quoted in Alex J. Pollock and Edward J. Pinto, "Federal Housing Regulators Have Learned and Forgotten Everything," *Law & Liberty*, Dec. 17, 2021, pp. 2–3.

8. An important result of house price inflation has been its differential impact on lower income households. The AEI Housing Center demonstrated that the spiked punch bowl inflated the prices of lower-priced houses more than others, crowding out low-income potential buyers. By policies that result in house price inflation, government actions, as they do in many other examples, generate unintended and unanticipated consequences.

9. Paul A. Volcker, *Keeping At It*, 2018, p. 224.

10. 2020 OFR Annual Report, p. 75.

11. Peter Grant, "Ladder Capital and Other Nonbank Lenders See a Boom," *Wall Street Journal* Sept. 29, 2021.

Chapter 9 · Municipal Debt in Covid Times

1. Barb Rosewicz, Justin Theal, and Alexandre Fall, "State Tax Revenue Passes a Recovery Milestone," *pewtrusts.org*, May 7, 2021.

2. Jimmy Vielkind, "States Are Swimming in Cash Thanks to Booming Tax Revenue and Federal Aid," *Wall Street Journal*, Jan. 22–23, 2021.

3. "Debt after COVID," Moody's Investors Service, June 2021.

4. David Beers et al., "BoC-BoE Sovereign Default Database: What's new in 2021?" Bank of England, p. 4.

5. Hannah Meisel, "Illinois Sees First Credit Rating Upgrade in Two Decades," *Illinois Newsroom*, June 30, 2021.

6. Ibid.

7. "Quarterly Summary of State and Local Government Tax Revenue for Third Quarter 2020," United States Census Bureau, Dec. 17, 2020.

8. Steve Bittenbender, "Sales Tax Revenues in New York Dropped by 10 Percent in 2020," *The Center Square*, Feb. 2, 2021.

9. Nick Reisman, "Sales Tax Revenue in New York Grows by More Than 57%," Spectrum Local News, June 16, 2021; also see "States Are Swimming in Cash," *WSJ*.

10. "Municipal bankruptcy: a primer on Chapter 9," *Nuveen*, Oct. 2021, which adds that since the institution of Chapter 9 in 1934, there have been about 700 municipal bankruptcy filings.

11. Cooper Howard, "Why Widespread Muni Defaults Are Unlikely to Happen," Charles Schwab advisorperspectives.com Feb. 4, 2021.

12. Andrea Riquier, "Municipal defaults are creeping up, suggesting more bondholder pain to come," *The Tell, MarketWatch*, Oct. 11, 2021.

13. "City of Chicago 2022 Budget Analysis," Office of Financial Analysis, Chicago City Council, 2021.

14. Ibid.

15. Hazel Bradford, "Puerto Rico Has 'Catastrophic' Levels of Debt—Report," *Pensions & Investments*, Crain Communications, Aug. 21, 2018.

16. Mary Williams Walsh, "How Puerto Rico is Grappling with a Debt Crisis," *New York Times*, May 16, 2017.

17. Danica Coto, "Puerto Rico Rejects Key Deal with Creditors to Reduce Debt," usnews.com, Feb. 23, 2021.

18. Ibid.

19. Amelia Cheatham, "Puerto Rico: A U.S. Territory in Crisis," *Council on Foreign Relations*, Nov. 25, 2020.

20. Ibid.

Chapter 10 · Pension Plans: Some Dubious Promises

1. 2021 FSOC Annual Report, p. 111.

2. Private Pension Plan Bulletin, 2018 data, U.S. Department of Labor, Jan. 2021.

3. FY 2020 Projections Report, Pension Benefits Guaranty Corporation, p. 8.

4. FY 2019 Projections Report, Pension Benefits Guaranty Corporation, p. 2.

5. Ibid., p. 1.

6. Alex J. Pollock, "Multi-Employer Pension Bailout Needs a Good Bank/Bad Bank Strategy,"*RealClearMarkets*, July 10, 2019.

7. FY 2020 Projection Report, Pension Benefits Guaranty Corporation, p. 3.

8. Robert Perry, David Pixley, and Jackson Lewis P.C., "Multiemployer Pension Plan Reform/Bailout May Be Greater Than Expected; Guidance Still Forthcoming," *JD Supra*, June 7, 2021.

9 Charles Blahous, "The American Rescue Plan's Disastrous Pension Bailout," *Mercatus.org*, April 19, 2021.

10. 2020 OFR Annual Report, p. 63.

11. "The State Pension Funding Gap: Plans Have Stabilized in Wake of Pandemic," *pewtrusts.org*, Sept. 14, 2021.

12. 2020 FSOC Annual Report, p. 113.

13. American Rescue Plan Act of 2021, Section 9901(c)(2)(B).

14. "Coronavirus State and Local Fiscal Recovery Funds Frequently Asked Questions," United States Department of the Treasury, Section 8.1, July 19, 2021.

15. Ibid.

16. 31 CFR Part 35 Jan. 6, 2022.

17. For 2020, Moody's used a 2.7 percent discount rate while Illinois used a rate close to seven percent.

18. Adam Shuster, "Moody's Report: Illinois Pension Debt Reaches Record-High $317 Billion," *illinoispolicy.org*, March 5, 2021. Shuster puts Illinois pension debt at $317 billion using Moody's methodology. Others, using the same methodology, place it at $313 billion. We have used the smaller number.

19. Ted Dabrowski and John Klingner, "Illinois pension shortfall surpasses $500 billion, average debt burden now $110,000 per household," *wirepoints.org*, Nov. 2021.

20. "The State Pension Funding Gap," *pewtrusts.org*.

21. Ted Dabrowski and John Klingner, "Pensions 101: Understanding Illinois' Massive Government-Worker Pension Crisis," *illinoispolicy.org* (sourced on Aug. 8, 2021).

22. "Pension Brief: Single-Employer Pension Plans Are Straining Illinois Municipalities' Credit Quality," S&P Global Ratings, July 7, 2021.

23. Dabrowski and Klingner, "Illinois pension shortfall surpasses $500 billion."

24. "Pension Brief," S&P Global Ratings.

25. Dabrowski and Klingner, "Pensions 101."

26. "Pension Brief," S&P Global Ratings.

27. Adam Andrzejewski, "Why Illinois Is in Trouble—109,881 Public Employees With $100,000+ Paychecks Cost Taxpayers $14B," *Forbes*, April 27, 2020.

Chapter 11 · Student Loans: A Failed Government Lending Program

1. Josh Mitchell, *The Debt Trap*, 2021, pp. 4–5, 7.
2. Ibid., pp. 28–29.
3. Volcker, *Keeping At It*, p. 53.
4. "Obama Cites Student Loan Savings," CBS News, March 27, 2010.
5. Zack Friedman, "Biden Says Student Loans May Cause Major Loss," *Forbes*, June 8, 2021.
6. "Government Student Loan Losses Mount," *Wall Street Journal*, Jan. 13, 2022.
7. Josh Mitchell, "Is the U.S. Student Loan Program Facing a $500 Billion Hole? One Banker Thinks So," *Wall Street Journal*, April 29, 2021.
8. Adam Looney, "Putting Student Loan Forgiveness in Perspective: How costly is it and who benefits?" Brookings Institution, Feb. 12, 2021.
9. Richard Fossey, *The Student-Loan Catastrophe*, 2017, p. 2.
10. Alex J. Pollock, "A New Housing Finance Option in the USA: MPF vs. MBS," *Housing Finance International*, March 1999.
11. "Thoughts on Student Loans," private memorandum, 2015.
12. Nassim Nicholas Taleb, *Skin in the Game*, 2018, p. 4.
13. Alex J. Pollock, "Colleges need to have skin in the game to tackle student loan debt," *The Hill*, May 7, 2019.
14. Alex first proposed this idea in 2012.
15. Mitchell, *The Debt Trap*, pp. 211–2.
16. Ibid., p. 217
17. Richard K. Vedder, "New Research Shows Federal Student Aid Is Worse than We Thought," James G. Martin Center for Academic Renewal, Dec. 11, 2019.

Chapter 12 · Central Banking to the Max

1. Walter Bagehot, *Lombard Street*, 1873, Hyperion Press 1962 edition, p. 85.
2. Bill-brokers being financial intermediaries who buy and sell short-term debt (bills), using money borrowed on the security of the bills to finance their inventory.
3. Walter Bagehot, *Lombard Street*, p. 88.
4. Ibid., p. 99.
5. Ibid., p. 101.
6. James Grant, *Bagehot*, 2019, pp. 171, 178.
7. In finance, a "put" is a right of the owner of an asset to offload that asset to another party if it becomes unprofitable. In this case, it means that the market can offload losses to the Fed.

8. Ben Bernanke, "The Economic Outlook and Monetary and Fiscal Policy," Testimony before the House Committee on the Budget, Feb. 9, 2011 (italics added).

9. 2021 OFR Annual Report, p. 40.

10. Monetization means the central bank buys the government bonds with newly created money, instead of private investors buying the bonds with savings. This inflates the money supply, credit and prices.

11. Nick Timiraos, "Fed Steps Up Deliberations on Shrinking Its $9 Trillion Asset Portfolio," *Wall Street Journal*, Jan. 25, 2022.

12. Richard Nixon, "Address to the Nation Outlining a New Economic Policy," Aug. 15, 1971.

13. Benn Steil, *The Battle of Bretton Woods*, 2013, p. 337.

14. Private presentation, quoted with permission.

Chapter 13 · Reflections on the Surprises of the Covid Crisis

1. Charles Goodhart and Manoj Pradhan, *The Great Demographic Reversal—Ageing Societies, Waning Inequality, and an Inflation Revival*, 2020, p. 214.

2. Lawrence H. Summers, "The Biden stimulus is admirably ambitious. But it brings some big risks, too," *Washington Post*, Feb. 4, 2021.

3. William H. McNeill, *Plagues and Peoples*, 1976, p. 168; and Kelsey Piper, "Here's how Covid-19 ranks among the worst plagues in history," Vox, Jan. 11, 2021.

4. Albert Edwards quoted by Gary Howes, "New Zealand Leads the 'Epic' Housing Bubble Rankings, Canada and the U.K. are Not Far Behind," *Pound Sterling Live*, Jun. 25, 2021.

5. Ibid.

6. Dalio, *Principles for Dealing with the Changing World Order*, pp. 136–7.

7. Graham Allison, *Destined for War*, 2017, p. 184.

8. David Halberstam, *The Coldest Winter*, 2007, p. 634.

Epilogue

1. David R. Kotok, "Two Links & a Rant: Tax-Free Munis, Quantitative Tightening, & Trolls in the Media," Cumberland Advisors, May 11, 2022.

2. Mona Ali, "Regime Change?" *Phenominalworld.org*, April 27, 2022.

3. Emily Flitter and David Yaffe-Bellany, "Russia Could Use Cryptocurrency to Blunt the Force of U.S. Sanctions," *The New York Times*, Feb. 23, 2022.

4. See for example, "Central Bank Digital Currency—Efficient Innovation or the End of the Private Banking System?" Federalist Society Webinar, May 10, 2022.

5. Agustin Carstens, "The Return of Inflation," SUERF Policy Note, April 2022.

6. See Alex J. Pollock, "Can the Federal Reserve Stop Being the World's Biggest Savings & Loan," *Housing Finance International*, Spring 2022.

7. Using the iShares 20+ Year Treasury Bond ETF (TLT) price

8. "Hide Away," *Almost Daily Grant's*, May 6, 2022.

9. Scott Chipolina, "Crypto market value tumbles $1.6 trillion since hitting November high," *Financial Times*, May 10, 2022.

10. May 12 and May 13, 2022, respectively.

11. See "One of the most popular cryptocurrencies loses 95% of its value in just a few days. Now it's hardly worth anything," *Crast.net*, May 11, 2022; and "Terra (LUNA), Terra (UST) Crash News: 99% down!" *Financial Express*, May 12, 2022.

12. "Toomey Announces Legislation to Create Responsible Regulatory Framework for Stablecoins," U.S. Senate Committee on Banking, Housing, and Urban Affairs, April 6, 2022; Proposal for a Regulation of the European Parliament and of the Council on Markets in Crypto-assets, and amending Directive (EU) 2019/1937, The European Commission, originally introduced in September 2020, as voted on by the European Union Parliament's Committee on Economic and Monetary Affairs, March 14, 2022.

13. Heather Gillers, "Inflation Raises Expenses for Pension Funds," Wall Street Journal, March 1, 2022.

14. May 11, 2022.

15. Claire Ballentine and Ella Ceron, "Don't Bother Paying Off Student Loan Debt Right Now, Advisers Say," *Bloomberg*, May 10, 2022.

16. "Rumors of Stagflation," *Wall Street Journal*, April 29, 2022.

17. "Treasuries fall as traders price in big US rates rise," quoting Alex Roever of JPMorgan, *Financial Times*, May 3, 2022.

18. "Central banks must play economic manoeuvres in the dark," *Financial Times*, May 7–8, 2022.

Bibliography

Adler, Howard B. and Alex J. Pollock. "Why a Fed Digital Dollar Is a Bad Idea." *RealClearMarkets*, 22 July 2021.

Allison, Graham. *Destined for War: Can America and China Escape Thucydides Trap?* Boston—New York: Houghton Mifflin Harcourt, 2017.

Areddy, James T. "China Creates Its Own Digital Currency, a First for Major Economy," *Wall Street Journal*, 5–6 April 2021.

Auer, Raphael, Jon Frost, Leonardo Gambacorta, Cyril Monnet, Tara Rice, and Hyun Song Shin. "Central Bank Digital Currencies: Motives, Economic Implications and the Research Frontier." Bank for International Settlements Working Papers, no. 976, Nov. 2021.

Bagehot, Walter. *Lombard Street: A Description of the Money Market*. Westport: Hyperion Press, 1962, originally published in 1873.

Bank for International Settlements. "Triennial Central Bank Survey of Foreign Exchange and Over-the-counter (OTC) Derivatives Markets in 2019." 8 December 2019.

Beers, David, Elliot Jones, Zacharie Quiviger, and John Walsh. "BoC–BoE Sovereign Default Database: What's new in 2021?" Staff Analytical Notes 2021-15, Bank of Canada, June 2021.

Bernanke, Ben S. Testimony before the U.S. House of Representatives Committee on the Budget. "The Economic Outlook and Monetary and Fiscal Policy." 9 Feb. 2011.

Blahous, Charles. "The American Rescue Plan's Disastrous Pension Bailout." *Mercatus.org*, 19 April 2021.

Boar, Codruta, and Andreas Wehrli. "Ready, steady, go?—Results of the third BIS survey on central bank digital currency." Bank for International Settlements Papers, no. 114, Jan. 2021.

Board of Governors of the Federal Reserve System. "Money and Payments: The U.S. Dollar in the Age of Digital Transformation." Jan. 2022.

Carr, Douglas. "How Deficit 'Stimulus' Supercharged Inflation." *National Review*, 23 Dec. 2021.

Cascaldi-Garcia, Danilo, Cisil Sarisoy, Juan M. Londono, John Rogers, Deepa Datta, Thiago Ferreira, Olesya Grishchenko, Mohammad R. Jahan-Parvar, Francesca Loria, Sai Ma, Marius Rodriguez, and Ilknur Zer. "What is Certain about Uncertainty?" International Finance Discussion Papers 1294. Washington: Board of Governors of the Federal Reserve System, https://doi.org/10.17016/IFDP.2020.1294. July 2020.

Cheatham, Amelia. "Puerto Rico: A U.S. Territory in Crisis." *Council on Foreign Relations*, 25 Nov. 2020.

Chicago City Council, Office of Financial Analysis. "City of Chicago 2022 Budget Analysis." 20 Sep. 2021.

Congress.gov. "Text - H.R.1319 - 117th Congress (2021–2022): American Rescue Plan Act of 2021." 11 March 2021. https://www.congress.gov/bill/117th-congress/house-bill/1319/text.

Congressional Research Service. *COVID-19 Impact on the Banking Industry: Conditions in the Second Quarter of 2020* (IN11500). Prepared by David W. Perkins and Raj Gnanarajah. Sept. 10, 2020.

Dabrowski, Ted, and John Klingner. "Illinois pension shortfall surpasses $500 billion, average debt burden now $110,000 per household." *wirepoints.org*, Nov. 2021.

———. "Pensions 101: Understanding Illinois' Massive Government-Worker Pension Crisis." *illinoispolicy.org*, sourced on 8 Aug. 2021.

Dalio, Ray. *Principles for Dealing with the Changing World Order*. New York, NY: Avid Read Press, 2021.

Diem White Paper, April 2020.

Employee Benefits Security Administration, U. S. Department of Labor. *Private Pension Plan Bulletin*. Abstract of 2018 Form 5500 Annual Reports. Jan. 2021.

Federal Deposit Insurance Corporation. *Quarterly Banking Profile*, June 2021.

Federal Reserve Bank of New York. *Quarterly Report on Household Debt and Credit (2021: Q4)*, Feb. 2022.

Financial Stability Board. "Policy Proposals to Enhance Money Market Fund Resilience." 30 June 2021.

Financial Stability Oversight Council (FSOC), 2021 Annual Report.

———. 2020 Annual Report.

———. 2019 Annual Report.

FINMA (Swiss Financial Market Supervisory Authority). "Libra Association: FINMA licensing process initiated." Press Release, 16 April 2020.

Fossey, Richard. *The Student-Loan Catastrophe: Postcards From the Rubble.* CreateSpace Independent Publishing Platform, 2017.

Goodhart, Charles, and Manoj Pradhan. *The Great Demographic Reversal: Ageing Societies, Waning Inequality, and an Inflation Revival.* London: Palgrave Macmillan, 2020.

Grant, James. *Bagehot: The Life and Times of the Greatest Victorian.* New York: W. W. Norton & Company, 2019.

———. "Memo to Morgan Stanley." *Grant's Interest Rate Observer,* 20 Sep. 2013.

Grantham, Jeremy. "Let the Wild Rumpus Begin: (Approaching the End of) The First U.S. Bubble Extravaganza: Housing, Equities, Bonds, and Commodities." *GMO.com, Viewpoints,* 20 Jan. 2022.

Halberstam, David. *The Coldest Winter: America and the Korean War.* New York: Hyperion, 2007.

Hayek, Friedrich August. *New Studies in Philosophy, Politics, Economics and the History of Ideas.* Chicago: University of Chicago Press, 1978.

Kay, John, and Mervyn King. *Radical Uncertainty: Decision-Making Beyond the Numbers.* New York: W. W. Norton & Company, 2020.

Keynes, John Maynard, *The General Theory of Employment,*1937.

Libra White Paper, 18 June 2019.

Looney, Adam. "Putting Student Loan Forgiveness in Perspective: How costly is it and who benefits?" Brookings Institution, *Up Front* blog, 12 Feb. 2021.

McCaffrey, Paul. "Annie Duke and Morgan Housel: Three Tools for Navigating Risk and Uncertainty." *CFAInstitute.org,* 6 June 2020.

McDonald, Oonagh. *Cryptocurrencies: Money, Trust and Regulation.* Newcastle upon Tyne: Agenda Publishing, 2021.

Mitchell, Josh. *The Debt Trap: How Student Loans Became a National Catastrophe.* New York: Simon & Schuster, 2021.

McNeill, William H. *Plagues and Peoples.* New York: Anchor Books, 1976.

Moody's Investor Service, "Debt after COVID: Focus On Sovereign Debt: Unequal Debt Realities." June 2021.

Nixon, Richard. "Address to the Nation Outlining a New Economic Policy." 15 Aug. 1971.

Office of Financial Research. Annual Report to Congress 2021. 17 Nov. 2021.

———. Annual Report to Congress 2020. 18 Nov. 2020

Paulson, Henry M. *On the Brink: Inside the Race to Stop the Collapse of the Global Financial System.* New York: Business Plus, 2010.

Pinto, Edward J., and Tobias Peter. "AEI housing market indicators, December 2021." AEI Housing Center, *AEIdeas,* 4 Jan. 2022.

Pollock, Alex J. "A New Housing Finance Option in the USA: MPF vs. MBS." *Housing Finance International*. London, Vol. 13, Iss. 3, March 1999.

———. "Can the Federal Reserve Stop Being the World's Biggest Savings & Loan," Housing Finance International, Spring 2022.

———. "Colleges need to have skin in the game to tackle student loan debt." *The Hill*, 7 May 2019.

———. "Fannie and Freddie Are Obviously SIFIs." Testimony before the U. S. Senate Committee on Banking, Housing, and Urban Affairs. Hearing on "Should Fannie Mae and Freddie Mac be Designated as Systemically Important Financial Institutions?" 25 June 2019.

———. *Finance and Philosophy: Why We're Always Surprised.* Philadelphia: Paul Dry Books, 2018.

———. "Multi-Employer Pension Bailout Needs a Good Bank/Bad Bank Strategy." *RealClearMarkets*, 10 July 2019.

———. "On Being Surprised (While Treasury Secretary)." *AEIdeas*, 18 Nov. 2010.

Pollock, Alex J., and Jay Brinkmann. "Homeownership Rates: It depends on whether you are married." *Housing Finance International*, Autumn 2016.

Pollock, Alex J., Hashim Hamandi, and Ruth Leung. "Banking Credit System, 1970–2020." Office of Financial Research Blog, 6 Jan. 2021.

Pollock, Alex J. and Edward J. Pinto. "Federal Housing Regulators Have Learned and Forgotten Everything." *Law & Liberty*, 17 Dec. 2021.

President's Working Group on Financial Markets. "Overview of Recent Events and Potential Reform Options for Money Market Funds." 22 Dec. 2020.

President's Working Group on Financial Markets, the Federal Deposit Insurance Corporation, and the Office of the Comptroller of the Currency. "Report on Stablecoins." Nov. 2021.

Powell, Jerome. Testimony before the U.S. Senate Committee on Banking, Housing, and Urban Affairs. Hearing on "The Semiannual Monetary Policy Report to the Congress," 23 Feb. 2021.

Rosewicz, Barb, Justin Theal, and Alexandre Fall. "State Tax Revenue Passes a Recovery Milestone: In Most States and Nationwide, Collections Overcome Early Pandemic Losses." *pewtrusts.org*, 7 May 2021.

S&P Global Ratings. "Pension Brief: Single-Employer Plans Are Straining Illinois Municipalities' Credit Quality," 7 July 2021.

Securities and Exchange Commission. "Money Market Fund Reforms," Rel. No. IC-34441, 15 Dec. 2021.

Selgin, George. *The Menace of Fiscal QE.* Washington, D.C.: Cato Institute, 2020.

Shuster, Adam. "Moody's Report: Illinois Pension Debt Reaches Record-High $317 Billion." *illinoispolicy.org*, 5 March 2021.

Steil, Benn. *The Battle of Bretton Woods: John Maynard Keynes, Harry Dexter White, and the Making of a New World Order.* Princeton: Princeton University Press, 2013.

Summers, Lawrence H. "The Biden stimulus is admirably ambitious. But it brings some big risks, too." *Washington Post*, 4 Feb. 2021.

Taleb, Nassim Nicholas. *Skin in the Game: Hidden Asymmetries in Daily Life.* New York: Random House, 2018.

Tucker, Paul. "The Repertoire of Official Sector Interventions in the Financial System: Last Resort Lending Market-Making, and Capital." Speech given at the Bank of Japan 2009 International Conference, Tokyo, 28 May 2009.

U.S. Census Bureau. "Quarterly Summary of State and Local Tax Revenue for Third Quarter 2020." 17 Dec. 2020.

U.S. Department of the Treasury. "Coronavirus State and Local Fiscal Recovery Funds Frequently Asked Questions." 19 July 2021.

U.S. Department of the Treasury, Board of Governors of the Federal Reserve System, Federal Reserve Bank of New York, U.S. Securities and Exchange Commission, and U.S. Commodity Futures Trading Commission. "Recent Disruptions and Potential Reforms in the U.S. Treasury Market: A Staff Progress Report." 8 Nov. 2021.

Vedder, Richard K. "New Research Shows Federal Student Aid Is Worse Than We Thought." James G. Martin Center for Academic Renewal, 11 Dec 2019.

Volcker, Paul A., and Christine Harper. *Keeping At It: The Quest for Sound Money and Good Government.* New York: PublicAffairs, 2018.

White, Lawrence H. "Should We Fear Stablecoins?" *Cato at Liberty* blog, Cato Institute, 24 June 2021.

White, William R. Comments at "The 2008 Global Financial Crisis in Retrospect" conference, Reykjavik, 2019.

———. "Conducting Monetary Policy in a Complex, Adaptive Economy: Past Mistakes and Future Possibilities." *Credit and Capital Markets*, Vol. 50, Iss. 2, Feb. 2017.

Index

Adler, Howard, 3
Alexander, Lamar, 157
Allison, Graham, 185
American Rescue Plan Act
  bailout of Illinois and, 128–129
  municipal bond market and, 126
  pension plans and, 133, 139–140,
    142, 143
Angell, Norman, 185, 186
Asset price boom of 2020-21,
  52–62
  banking industry and, 94
  ending of, 61–62
  GameStop shares and, 60–61
  housing market and, 52–56, 59
  inflation and, 59–60
  interest rates and, 56–59
  interventions causing, 177–178
  risks created by, 94

Bagehot, Walter, 182
  on central bank handling of crises,
    30, 160–163
Bailouts
  approach to, 139–140
  in April 2020, 9
  from central banks, debate over,
    160–165
  Cincinnatian Doctrine and, 9–10,
    165–166, 181

  Cincinnatian Problem and, 165,
    174, 181–182
  municipal bond markets and, 126
  for states' pension fund deficits,
    128–129, 133, 147–148
  winding down of emergency pro-
    grams and, 165
Banking credit system, 109
Banking industry, 92–105
  asset price inflation and, 94
  bank failures and, 94–97
  bank stock price drop and, 93
  capital and liquidity requirements
    for, 28
  CECL standard and, 102–104
  commercial real estate and, 26, 100
  consumer debt and, 101
  corporate lending by, 97–100
  countercyclical policies and,
    104–105
  Covid-19 pandemic and, 13–14,
    28, 92–94
  deposit increases and, 95
  global systemically important
    banks and, 95–96
  loan loss reserves and, 92–93,
    101–104, 178, 202n.1
  mortgage lending shift away from,
    117
Bank of Canada, assets of, 169–170

215

Municipal Liquidity Facility
  (MLF), 35, 125–126, 133
Mutual funds
  bond, redemption problems and,
    44–45
  Covid-19 pandemic and, 16
  Money Market Mutual Fund
    Liquidity Facility and, 35

Natural gas prices, increase in,
  59–60
Negative interest rates, 59
New York City, pension fund prob-
  lems in, 133
New York Metropolitan Transporta-
  tion Authority, borrowing from
  MLF by, 125–126
Nixon, Richard, U.S. move to fiat
  currency and, 70, 172–176
Nonbank mortgage companies, 117

Obama, Barack, 152
Office of Financial Research, on
  financial stability reports, 7
Oil prices, increase in, 59
On the Crisis (Paulson), 6

Pandemics
  Covid-19. *See* Covid-19 pandemic
  next, future financial crises and,
    184
Park District Pension Fund, 145
Paulson, Henry, 6
Paycheck Protection Program
  (PPP), 32, 99
Paycheck Protection Program
  Liquidity Facility, 35
Peel, Robert, 161
Pension Benefit Guaranty Corpora-
  tion, 136–141, 158, 179
Pension funds, 134–149
  bailout of, 178–179

deficits in, 128–129, 133, 193
defined, 134
funded ratio of, 135
interest rates and, 134
multiemployer, 135, 136–141,
  178–179
PBGC and, 136–141, 158, 179
persistence of deficits in, 193
private single-employer, 135
public, 135, 141–149
Philadelphia, pension fund problems in, 133
Pollock, Alex, 3
  on banking credit system, 109
  on financial cycles, 104
  MPF program and, 156
  on multiemployer pension plans,
    138
Powell, Jerome, 72, 86
Pradhan, Manoj, 177
President's Working Group on
  Financial Markets (PWG)
  on liquidity problems faced by
    money market funds, 47–49
  on stablecoins, 73, 82
Primary Dealer Credit Facility, 35
Primary Market Corporate Credit
  Facility, 35
*Principles of Dealing with the
  Changing World Order* (Dalio),
  70–71
Pritzker, J. B., 147
Puerto Rico, debt crisis of, 130–133
Puerto Rico Oversight, Manage-
  ment, and Economic Stability
  Act (PROMESA), 131

Quantitative Easing (QE)
  Bank of Japan and, 167–168
  Federal Reserve and, 164–165
Quantitative Tightening (QT), 120

Alex J. Pollock is a Senior Fellow of the Mises Institute and the author of *Finance and Philosophy: Why We're Always Surprised* (Paul Dry Books) and *Boom and Bust: Financial Cycles and Human Prosperity*. He was Principal Deputy Director of the Office of Financial Research, U.S. Treasury, from November 2019 to February 2021, and has been a fellow of the R Street Institute and the American Enterprise Institute, president and CEO of the Federal Home Loan Bank of Chicago, and a director of CME Group, Ascendium Education Group, and the Great Books Foundation. Pollock's work includes the study of financial systems and their recurring crises; the politics of finance, risk, and uncertainty; central banking; and housing finance. He is a graduate of Williams College, the University of Chicago, and Princeton University, and he lives in Lake Forest, Illinois.

Howard B. Adler is an attorney and former government official. From May 2019 through January 2021, he served as Deputy Assistant Secretary of the Treasury for the Financial Stability Oversight Council, where he was responsible for monitoring the financial stability of the United States during the first year of the Covid-19 crisis. He was awarded the Treasury's Distinguished Service Award for his efforts by the Secretary of the Treasury. Mr. Adler was a partner for over thirty years in the Gibson, Dunn & Crutcher, LLP law firm, where he served as co-head of both the firm's Corporate Transactional Practice Group and REIT Practice Group. Prior to joining Gibson Dunn, he served as Executive Vice President and General Counsel of The Riggs National Bank of Washington, D.C. Mr. Adler has also served as the Treasurer of the Washington, D.C. Bar and on the Board of Governing Trustees of American Ballet Theatre. He is a graduate of Johns Hopkins University and New York University School of Law, and he lives in the Washington, D.C. area.